DEVELOP YOUR
POWER TO DEAL
WITH PEOPLE

BENTLEY BARNABAS

Develop Your Power to Deal With People

PARKER PUBLISHING COMPANY, INC.   West Nyack, N.Y.

PRINTED IN THE UNITED STATES OF AMERICA
ISBN-0-13-205450-7
B & P

To
John C. Peterson, Ph.D.
1884–1968
In Grateful Memory

A WORD FROM
THE AUTHOR

This book provides a practical, down-to-earth way to develop your power to get other people to do what you want them to do. It shows you how to "put yourself across" to others.

The book provides a "bridge" from the proved principles derived from research and observation. to the very practical situations of everyday life. The principles are translated into real-life illustrations, examples and case histories. While Chapter 1 deals with general principles derived from modern psychology, each ensuing chapter provides additional fundamentals but also links them to actions, words, phrases which make those fundamentals "come alive." They can help you develop your Power to deal with people.

Real-Life Examples

For example, Chapter 2 shows the five ways in which you make your personal Stimulus stronger in its impact on another person. The Chapter concludes with an actual interview in which a successful person demonstrates each of the five ways in a real-life incident. The narrative contains annotations to link each action or phrase to one of the five ways described earlier.

Then, in Chapter 3, we first show how important it can be to tie something you want to "put across" to the specific background or "way of life" of the other person. We show that such a linkage "multiplies" the power to deal with another person.

Then we provide four clear-cut and detailed examples of this powerful effect in action. Two are from actual sales situations, two from supervisory situations.

Examples From Sales, Supervisory And "Personal" Situations

Chapters 4, 5, and 6 contain proven techniques for getting others to accept your ideas. There is a total of 19 such ways to "smooth the pathway" for acceptance of an idea or course of action. For each of the 19 techniques there are two or three examples under separate headings for "The Supervisory Situation," "The Sales Situation" and the "Personal Or Home Situation." There are well over 100 such examples to give you a clear, concise understanding of how to put your ideas and yourself across to others.

The Crucial Situation—Overcoming Resistance

Chapters 7, 8, 9, and 10 deal with the critical situation that arises when you meet with resistance to your ideas or you need to get someone to give up what you feel is a "wrong" idea or attitude. Again, the techniques are explained and each is followed by examples from sales, supervisory or personal-home situations. More than a hundred examples are provided.

Handling "Problem" Personalities

When you reach Chapter 11 you'll have an opportunity to develop insight into certain types of personalities that provide "problems" to others, including yourself. You'll learn the fundamentals of "how they got that way" and how to understand and deal with them.

Getting People To Remember You

Part of developing Power to deal with people involves establishing your identity and getting people to remember you.

Again, the fundamentals are illustrated by examples of successful people and how they accomplished this end.

"To Get The Most Out Of This Chapter"

Each Chapter includes memory-aids to be sure that you learn the techniques and principles and how to use them. These are covered at the end of each chapter under the heading "To Get The Most Out Of This Chapter." You'll find that they will not only be easy to do, but they'll be fun, too!

Examples Through All Chapters

Whether you're learning how to "put yourself across" through clarity of expression or learning how to build attitudes that build up your Power, examples make clear to you how to do it.

Techniques Tested By Actual Seminars

The things you will learn from this book are not theoretical or academic. They have been tested and proved by 477 persons who participated in 24 seminar sessions which I conducted over a period of years. Eleven different companies sponsored these seminars for sales, supervisory or public-contact employees. In many cases top management participated. Five of the companies sponsored "repeat" programs and one company has repeated the program seven times!

You can feel confident that the material in the book is useful and valuable because it has been "through the mill." The 477 people who found it helped them develop Power in dealing with people were of all types. They consisted of 160 men in high-level sales work, 276 executives and supervisors, and 41 public-contact personnel.

So, whether your goal is success in selling, supervising others, becoming a community leader, or just being a happier person as a result of obtaining acceptance for yourself and your ideas, you'll find this book a valuable tool. If you have the motivation to learn how to develop Power in dealing with people—you'll benefit from this book.

Bentley Barnabas

ACKNOWLEDGEMENTS

Because my own ideas and behavior have been conditioned by so many contacts, it would be impossible for me to give credit to the hundreds of human beings who have had their influence on me and, thus, on the writing of this book.

My father was a great salesman and sales manager and I learned much about dealing with people from things he did and said.

John Christian Peterson, Ph.D., (1884-1968) who sponsored me for graduate work in Industrial Psychology, has been the most potent influence in my life. For that reason, I have dedicated this book to his memory.

Irvin T. Shultz, Ph.D., now retired, but formerly of Friends University and Baylor University, had much to do with my growth in the field of psychology. The same is true of Bill Hercher, a colleague and co-builder of Associated Personnel Technicians, Inc.

Every one of the many clients that our Company has served in the past twenty-five years is entitled to my thanks for his contribution and his recognition of the fact that scientific psychology could improve the world of work.

Of these clients, The Coleman Company of Wichita, for whom I have been permitted to train over two hundred young men in techniques of dealing with people in supervisory situations, deserves prime credit. The Union National Bank of Wichita, The Atlas Finance Company (now merged with a larger company), and the S. A. Long Company gave me similar opportunities for both research and field study.

Companies, however, are really people. Thanks should be directed to such corporate principals as Sheldon Coleman, G. Lawrence Keller and Vernon Williams of The Coleman Company, and to Clarence Coleman, President of the Union National Bank along with Robert R. Snodgrass (deceased) of Atlas and Roy Wood (deceased) of The S. A. Long Company.

Thanks are also directed to Loma May of the Jam Handy Organization who has been a sound advisor and "sounding board," as well as to my sister, Gertrude E. Faucher, and my wife, Pearl.

10

CONTENTS

Principles Apply Broadly • Your New Approach: Learn the Principles and Apply Them • The Six Principles You Need to Know • Let's Dig a Little Deeper into Human Behavior • How Experience Results in Conditioning • "Needs"—An Important Word in Conditioning • Knowledge of Psychological Needs Essential in Learning About a Person • Conditioning Is a Part of Him • "The Pathways to the Mind..." Stimulate More Than One Sense Organ • The Need for a Feeling of Security • Differences in Means of Satisfying This Need • The Need for a Feeling of Personal Worth or Importance • How This Is Satisfied • Sometimes It's a Combination of the Two Needs • How to Avoid Acts Which Reduce Another's Feeling of Personal Worth •Detecting "False" Principles

"Mechanics" the Same as Create Conditioning • The Stimulus Is YOU • The Response—Action that Furthers Your Goals • Making Stimulus Strong Enough to Produce the "Real" Response • The Entryways— the Sense Organs • Ways to Make the Stimulus Stronger • Stimulating More Than One Sense

11

Chapter One

THE NEW WAY TO DEVELOP YOUR POWER
TO DEAL WITH PEOPLE

There is a *new* way for you to develop your Power to deal with people.

It does not involve the learning of catchy phrases. It is not a course in public speaking. It is not a series of "pep talks."

Moreover, this new way to develop your power to deal with people is not limited to selling. Nor does this new way limit your skill to just good supervision or building good industrial relations. It applies to *any* situation involving your effort to get other people to do what *you* want them to do.

Why is it *new?* It is new because each year we learn more about people and why they behave as they do. Each year the sciences of psychology, sociology, psychiatry, and even brain physiology are making new findings. While they seemed to disagree in the past, findings in recent years have brought them closer to unity. Certain *principles* about human behavior have emerged. Your new approach to power in dealing with people is based on these principles.

Principles Apply Broadly

The man to whom this book is dedicated—Dr. John C. Peterson—once said: "We have not really learned something until we have learned it at the level of principle." What did he mean? He meant that if we learned a principle we could apply it to any situation that arose. If we learn *how* to do something (like changing a tire) we have learned that one thing, no more. If we learn *why* we do something in a given way—if we learn the underlying principle involved—we can call on that knowledge whenever it would be useful. Such knowledge could apply and be useful in many situations.

A Simple Example

Let's say you're teaching me how to change a tire. As I start to tighten the lug nuts in the final phase, you see me rise on my tiptoes, straighten my arm, and prepare to put my full weight on the lug wrench. You stop me. You tell me to use the muscles of my arm, not my full weight. Now, if you tell me no more than that you have taught me how to tighten the lug nuts on a spare wheel. Nothing more.

If you say: "You see, Bentley, that wrench is a lever-arm and it multiplies your strength. Your full weight on the end of it could strip the threads on the nut or bolt. So just stand flat footed and use your arm muscles."

Now you have taught me something that applies every time I tighten a nut on a bolt or use the lever-arm principle to increase my power! You have taught me a principle that has broad application.

Your New Approach: Learn The Principles And Apply Them

This book is going to show principles that increase your power to deal with people. It is going to give you examples showing those principles in action.

You're going to learn *why* people behave as they do. That involves the broad principles. Then you're going to see *how* those principles apply to different situations.

The end result is Power to deal with people—not just in selling, not just in supervising, but in every relationship you have with others.

The Six Principles That You Need To Know

While there are many principles that have to do with the

findings of the behavioral sciences, there are six that you need to learn to develop power to deal with people. Let's list them and learn them, here and now. Even though they may sound academic, I promise you that you'll see how practical and valuable they are.

> *Principle #1.* People behave as they do because they have been *conditioned* by their experiences.
> *Principle #2.* Conditioning results from individual acts which satisfy human needs.
> *Principle #3.* Properly classified, human needs are simple, not complex.
> *Principle #4.* Everything you can learn about a person helps you to understand and predict his behavior.
> *Principle #5.* The human mind is a part of the human body and conditioning is physiological as well as mental.
> *Principle #6.* The pathways to the mind are through the sense organs.

Let's Dig A Little Deeper Into Human Behavior

Principle #1 is important because it explains why each person behaves as an individual, a unique entity. There are only two factors which make a person what he is at the time you deal with him. One is his inheritance—the capacities which, while latent and undeveloped, were present in the genes at his conception. The other factor is the sum of the things he has experienced throughout his life up to the time you came to deal with him.

Experience Results In Conditioning

The things each person experiences are stored up in his mind and brain. Each time some stimulus from his environment causes him to make a response which satisfies a need, a psychological and physiological change takes place which predisposes him to react in the same way when a similar stimulus is repeated. Several such repetitions result in "habit" or *conditioning*. This process, called "Stimulus-Response," creates a predisposition to behave in a certain way.

Psychologists have proved this conclusively with experiments on both people and animals. Just as important, Brain Physiologists have proved the psychological experiments by showing that conditioning actually results in a *chemical change in the nerve cells of the brain* and central nervous system.

Because the brain is so complex (with its ten billion—10,000,000,000—cells or "relays"), conditioning that takes place in one brain area may be shared or "relayed" to another area.

Thus Principle #1 is essential to developing power to deal with people—you need to consider each person as the result of his conditioning, his past experience.

"Needs"—An Important Word In Conditioning

This brings us to *Principle #2*—Conditioning results from acts which satisfy human needs. The word "needs" is important, for unless the response to a stimulus satisfies a "need," the psychological and physiological change does not take place. There is no predisposition to repeat, no conditioning. To the child, candy not only tastes good but adds to the supply of blood sugar which the active child needs. He becomes conditioned to want and like candy.

Properly Classified, "Needs" Are Simple
Not Complex (Principle #3)

You will find long lists of "needs" in many books dealing with psychology. Unfortunately, such long lists do not give you a *principle* that is easy to remember.

Human needs fall under two main headings:

Physiological Needs
Psychological Needs

However, in developing power to deal with people you will seldom work with their physiological needs. These are subordinated in modern life situations, especially with adults. Children may be persuaded to do things in order to get dessert or candy, for example. Adults would buy the candy if they felt the need for energy or desired something sweet!

Psychological Needs Are The Important Ones For You

The psychological needs are the ones we use in developing power to deal with people. Again, a long list is not needed. There are just two that are of primary importance in dealing with people:

The Need For A Feeling Of Security
The Need For A Feeling Of Personal Worth

These needs are always present, always capable of evoking a response. Of the two, Personal Worth (or Sense of Importance) is the more useful because it is always present, always dependable as a source of motivation. A person may feel secure and not threatened in certain areas and at certain times, but he always wants to feel important, worthy.

Remember this simple classification of human needs. It will help you to develop your Power to deal with people.

Knowledge Of These Needs Helps In Learning About A Person

Principle #4 says: "Everything you can learn about a person helps you to understand and predict his behavior." This principle came out of a graduate seminar session. Dr. Peterson asked the group to name characteristics or background information that would be of help in predicting behavior. As each of us mentioned something, he wrote it on the blackboard. The list became very long—politics, church affiliation, family, education—all of the things that could be learned about another human being.

Then he asked: "Can we make a generalization from this long list?"

I spoke up: "Anything you can learn about a person helps you to understand and predict his behavior."

Dr. Peterson's eyes twinkled. He did not accept the generalization and continued to look for someone who would volunteer another. Finally it came from another graduate student: *"Everything* you can learn about a person helps you to understand and predict his behavior." Just a difference of one word—but "everything" stated a better principle than "anything." As a matter of discipline, Dr. Peterson wanted us to be sure that we did not overlook something important that would help us to understand and predict human behavior.

Relates To Needs

Principle #4 is best understood if we go back to Principle #3. What makes this person feel secure? What makes him feel ten feet tall? What inspires his motivation to attain? Does he collect oil paintings or stamps?

The things he has done in the past provide clues to what makes him feel important, secure. Each little clue that you discover, each finding you make about him, tells you that he did something in the past that enhanced his feeling of security or his need for personal worth.

These findings tell you about his past conditioning. If you link your efforts to change him, to accept you or your ideas, to this past experience—earlier conditioning—you are developing Power to deal with him. This will be further discussed in Chapters Two and Three.

Principle #5: Conditioning Is A Part Of Him

Earlier we showed that brain experts had proved that conditioning is not just "habit" in the psychological sense, but that it also involves physiological changes of a chemical nature in the brain cells. Principle #5, "The human mind is a part of the human body and conditioning is physiological as well as mental," anchors this in your mind.

Why do I stress this? I want you to be fully aware of the fact that it is difficult to change this prior conditioning. It is a difficult task to change a "habit." It takes a strong stimulus, repeated in satisfaction of a need and repeated many times, to change prior conditioning. It is *set* in the nervous system. A chemical change has taken place.

There may be times when you will have to accomplish change very slowly because of this. Our primary emphasis, though, in telling you the ways to develop power, is in *using* the prior conditioning, not changing it. If you tie your efforts to the prior conditioning, if you learn "why" he behaves as he does, you will multiply your power to deal with him.

Principle #6: "The Pathways To The Mind..."

Principle #5 helps you realize that your Power will come from disciplining yourself to the psychological and physiological facts of conditioning. Now Principle #6 adds one further element of self-discipline: "The pathways to the mind are through the sense organs." There are no shortcuts. We have no scientific evidence that your brain can communicate directly with another brain by any "telepathy" or practical application of electronics or radionics. Perhaps some people will develop this capacity in the future, but for now you will have to live with the fact of Principle #6.

Sight, Sound, Touch, Taste, Smell

The five basic senses are the pathways to the mind. To learn, remember, become aware, a person must see, hear, touch, taste, or smell something. There is a sixth sense—the sense of balance in the middle ear—but it is not ordinarily useful in dealing with people. Most psychologists just classify the five senses—sight, sound, touch, taste, and smell.

Each of these senses conveys messages to the brain and central nervous system. These messages are called stimuli as they strike the sense organs. If the message is strong and calls for action, a response is the result. An "arcing" process takes place between the nerve cells that are linked to the sense organs and those (lying nearby) that are linked to the muscles. When this action satisfies a need and is repeated (reinforced), conditioning results.

More important: If the stimulus is linked to the prior conditioning process (through your knowledge of the person and his prior conditioning) it encounters less resistance and may find great receptivity.

Stimulate More Than One Sense Organ

Later we will discuss how a stimulus may be made stronger if it strikes more than one sense organ at the same time. Audiovisual (sight and sound simultaneously) stimuli produce greater likelihood of response and learning than just a sight or a sound. We will emphasize this repeatedly in practical ways later in this book.

Learn All Of These Principles

While I am not an exponent of rote learning, still I maintain that your Power will be greater if you memorize these Principles. They will cause your task of dealing with people to be easier, more certain, and more productive of behavior that will further your goals. They describe the disciplined process that has made successful people great. They learned that each person is different, that his needs made him that way, that people want security and to feel important, and that the more they learned *about* them the better they could deal *with* them. They did not express these principles in the same words I have used, but they learned them, nevertheless. You should do this, too.

More About "Needs"

Since conditioning results from acts (responses) that satisfy human needs, we should elaborate a little more on the two main Psychological Needs—the need for a feeling of Security and the need for a feeling of Personal Worth—importance. The things that we do to satisfy these two needs have a great deal to do with our life pattern—our life "style."

The Need For A Feeling Of Security

Because man is the only animal with a great and complex brain capable of storing millions of "bits" (a computer term) of information, he is able to look ahead. He can consider the future. No other animal can do it to the extent that man can.

Many unusual things about man come as a result of this endowment. Man is the only animal that is aware that he will die someday. This has created the life insurance business!

As a result of this ability to anticipate the future, man wants to feel secure about that future. He wants to safeguard himself and his family against reversals, contingencies, crises, and just plain wear and tear. This may be the need, the motivation, that causes him to learn a trade, save money, pay off a mortgage, feel the threat of inflation—yes, there are hundreds, even thousands of things that we do to satisfy our need for a feeling of security.

Difference In Means Of Satisfying This Need

There is no one total pattern of satisfying the need for security that is common to all individuals. Many people own life insurance, of course. Many others are home owners. After that, however, the satisfying of the need for a feeling of security becomes more highly individualized.

If you learn how and why an individual has satisfied this need, you have clues to the knowledge needed to apply Principle #4—"Everything you can learn about a person helps you to understand and predict his behavior."

The Need For A Feeling Of Personal Worth Or Importance

The need for a feeling of personal worth is even more important than the need for a feeling of security. At some times and under some circumstances a person feels very secure and will not be motivated by an appeal to this need. On the other hand, the need for a feeling of personal worth is always present.

Every person wants to feel important.

This Is Satisfied In Many Different Ways!

The need to feel important, worthy, is satisfied in so many ways that it would be impossible to list all of the things people do to satisfy it. One man collects paintings, another collects coins. One man takes pride in his golf score, another in his bowling score or his boat.

Fortunately, there are ways to find out some of the things a person does to satisfy his need for personal worth. As we will show in Chapter 3, the clues are unmistakable if you look for them. Sometimes they are found out by asking questions and listening, sometimes by looking up records, sometimes by asking others. We'll devote a lot of thought to that in later chapters.

Sometimes It's A Combination Of The Two Needs

We may buy a home and pay off the mortgage in order to satisfy our need for security, but at the same time we may buy it in a neighborhood that increases our personal worth. In buying a car we may add a safety feature in order to feel secure, buy a deluxe model because we take pride in the little crossed flags on the fender. We may buy one radio set in a beautiful cabinet to draw favorable comments from friends and another AM-FM battery set to be able to receive storm warnings when the electricity is off or lightning interferes with the AM signal!

This is why Principle #4 employs the word "everything" to describe what knowledge may be useful in analyzing another person's needs and predicting his behavior. Some little clue, apparently unimportant, may make it possible for you to use a special technique (Chapters Four, Five, Six) to get acceptance for you and your ideas. It may uncover a "multiplier" for your power in dealing with him as shown in Chapter Three.

Remember: Avoid Acts Which Reduce Another's Feeling of Personal Worth

An important aspect of developing Power in dealing with people is to avoid making an assault on another person's feeling of personal worth. In later chapters we will show specific ways to smooth the pathway for your ideas by linking your ideas to the other person's feeling of personal worth. In some extreme or unusual situations you may find it necessary to use "reverse English" and make him feel that he will lose personal worth if he does not accept your idea. Even when it becomes necessary to use this method, there is still no assault on his personal worth IF he accepts the idea. And, as we will show, these are the most difficult and "risky" techniques.

Nevertheless, the general rule is: Never make him feel "little." If you can make him feel "big" by accepting you and your ideas, you will be developing POWER.

Watch Out For "False" Principles

You may become exposed to some writers, teachers, or trainers who will utter principles that are "false." Some sales trainers make sweeping statements and imply that some techniques are universal. Principles are universal, but techniques are not. "Canned" presentations or stereotyped methods are *sure* to lose *some* sales. The mere fact that a certain type of presentation works in quite a few cases does not make it a safe procedure for the person who wants to develop Power.

Look out for sweeping statements that do not relate to a principle. We have shown sound principles in this chapter.

One sales trainer says: "Always make the customer a friend." If you adopt that attitude and make a lot of sales, your list of friends is going to be very long! But many of your customers don't want you for a friend—they want you as an effective consultant who understands their needs.

In some colleges they teach a course in "human relations" which tends to frighten the students by making them so cautious in dealing with people that they lose effectiveness. Such courses emphasize things *not* to do, but fail to tell you *what* to do. Negative principles are wrong unless they are the opposites of positive principles. If you learn the positive principles you don't need a list of "don'ts."

One young supervisor told me that his college course in human relations made him afraid to enter a face-to-face situation with a subordinate. Everybody liked him, but he lacked effectiveness. He had been led astray by a false principle: He thought that if people liked you, then they would do what you wanted them to do. He found out that this was not true.

Don't be afraid of dealing with people. Go at it intelligently and systematically in the ways we demonstrate in this book and you need not worry. You'll increase your Power.

Avoid Stereotypes

Forget any tendency you may have to stereotype people. If someone suggests that you classify people remember that people always differ because of differences in their conditioning (Principle #1). No two human beings have been subject to the same ranges and types of experience. No two have identical psychological needs.

If two people, or a group, have been made subject to some of the same experiences use that as a part of what you learn about them, but then look for the differences!

Get Rid Of Bias

Study yourself to free yourself from biases that may blind you to important differences in people. You may have had troubles with red-headed people, but it is not safe to say that they are hot-tempered. The evidence is to the contrary. Blondes are not necessarily harum-scarum, nor beautiful women "dumb." Stereotypes derived from your limited experience with people may prevent your search for the important things that motivate them and increase your Power to deal with them.

Keep your mind open. Look on each person you deal with as a challenge to your ability to learn about and understand him.

To Get The Most Out Of This Chapter

Throughout this book we will suggest things to do to get the most out of each chapter. Many of these suggestions will have to do with some action (response) which will "set" the knowledge in your mind and brain. You will be "conditioning" yourself.

For example, take paper and a pencil and write down the six Principles in this chapter.

As you do it, leave space between each Principle. Then go back and re-word that Principle in your own terms. For example, you might re-write Principle #1: "A person's experience causes him to become conditioned and that's why he behaves as he does."

Write out a list of your biases. Study them to see how your experience caused you to develop these attitudes toward types or classes of persons.

Write a list of the things that contribute to a satisfaction of your need for a feeling of security.

Write a list of the things that make you feel important, or that enhance your feeling of personal worth.

Do the same for someone you know personally—write down things that make him feel more secure and things that make him feel more important.

Chapter Two

HOW TO
CHANGE THE BEHAVIOR
OF OTHERS

Now that we have learned the "why" of human behavior—
why people behave as they do—our next step is to learn how
behavior is changed.

Whether you are a supervisor, a salesman, or a person who
wants to influence others in a general way, your success and
happiness will depend on *changing* others.

You must get others to accept your ideas and *act* on them. It
is not enough to get them to give lip service and agree with you
superficially. If you are to effect a change it involves
action . . . response.

In addition you must get them to give up "wrong" ideas or
negative attitudes and overcome the objections they raise to the
ideas that you advance.

The "Mechanics" Are The Same As Those
Which Create Conditioning

As you studied in Chapter One, you learned that behavior

originates when a stimulus produces a response. If the same stimulus produces the same response in satisfaction of a need, the individual becomes "conditioned." He is predisposed to act in the same way when that stimulus is repeated.

When we set out to change the behavior of another person, the same process is set in motion. We present a certain stimulus in the hope of getting a certain response.

The Stimulus Is YOU

The only difference between changing behavior and the ordinary stimulus response activity is that now *you* are the stimulus. It is not a hot stove, a loud noise, or a bright light. The stimulus is YOU.

It is not just one thing such as your voice, although that is very important—it is everything about you. That is why we capitalized the word YOU. It is the BIG YOU, not the little you.

Your voice, of course, is a prime stimulus when you deal with people. Your appearance, your expression, things that can be seen and pointed out are a part of your stimulus. And don't forget that the other persons with whom you deal have a sense of smell, too! Breath and body odor could be negative factors.

The main point is that YOU are the stimulus. If you're selling a product, its advantages are seen through your eyes. If you're selling an idea, the idea is perceived only through your expression of it.

The Response Is Action That Furthers Your Goals

The response is not just a "yes" or a "no." The fact that the person says "yes" or nods his head does not necessarily mean that he will carry through with what you want him to do. Many salesmen are puzzled because they received favorable response throughout a presentation, but were stopped "cold" when it came to getting the name on the order blank. The fact that he says "no" (he won't do it anymore) is no assurance that he won't revert to a wrong idea or attitude when you are not there.

The Stimulus Must Be Strong Enough to Produce The "Real" Response

The reason why we must carefully define that the response represents *action* stems from the need for a stronger stimulus to produce the "real" instead of the superficial response.

Hence we must investigate the ways in which you take steps to strengthen your stimulus.

Let's Go Back To Our "Principles"

We learned from Principle #1 that people behave as they do because they have been conditioned by their experience. Principle #2 showed that conditioning results from acts which satisfy needs and then (#3) that these needs are really only two—the need for security and the need for importance or personal worth. Principle #4 showed that by learning about a person, we could take steps toward understanding and predicting his behavior.

All of these Principles relate to the strengthening of the stimulus. The stimulus is stronger if it is individualized to the needs and background of the other person. We will devote Chapter 4 to this in detail. Your stimulus is stronger if it is related to needs—either from the past or for the future.

Principles #5 And #6 Must Be Kept In Mind

Going to our next step, the strengthening of your stimulus directed toward another person must take into account that the human mind lives in a human body. One great philosopher has even expressed the thought that the human mind is *imprisoned* in the human body. There is more to the mind than just the brain and central nervous system, but throughout life, the body is a "prison" which confines the mind.

Your approach to strengthening your stimulus must be disciplined to this unhappy limitation. The human mind is a part of the human body (Principle #5). We can only reach it through the pathways (senses and nerves) with which the body provides us (Principle #6).

There Are No "Short Cuts"

Sometimes when we travel over the earth we can take "short cuts" that save distance. We take a turnpike or freeway to save time and distance, but ordinarily we don't "cut across" fields. We usually cross rivers where there are bridges. It is the same way with the pathways to the mind. Our stimulus must travel nature's pre-designed routes.

The Entryways Are At The Sense Organs

The gateways to the mind, the entryways to the routes we must take to reach the central clearinghouse of ideas and actions are the sense organs. These are eyes, ears, skin, nose, and mouth. The nerve endings at those points receive sensations that cause us to have sight, hear sound, feel what is going on around us, smell, or taste things. There is a sixth sense organ—the semi-circular canals in the middle ear which give us our sense of balance—but this is more like an internal or "servo" mechanism. It tells us if we are rightside up or upside down, lying down or sitting up.

There are no other known ways by which a stimulus can reach the brain and central nervous system—the mind.

The Stimulus Must Be Strong As It
Reaches The Sense Organs

To make our stimulus more effective, we must first realize that it must be at full strength at the time it reaches the sense organs. While it may increase in power due to the great capacity of the other person's brain to exchange and share past experience throughout the various brain areas, the power that evokes any such "multiplying" influences originates in the sense organs first.

The Ways To Make The Stimulus Stronger

With these fundamentals behind us, let's look at the ways in which we can make our Stimulus stronger.

First, there is the obvious way: Make it strike the sense organ with greater impact. The stimulus that is louder to the ears, bigger to the eyes has a greater impact. While this is "obvious", it is seldom as useful as other ways.

Second, we strengthen the stimulus if we prepare it in such a way that it travels smoothly along the pathways to the mind. We design it in such a way that it gets greater receptivity in terms of its potential to satisfy needs.

Third, we make our stimulus stronger if we cause it to reach two sense organs at the same time.

Fourth, we may strengthen it by getting secondary stimulation of another sense organ at the brain level. We may not be able to stimulate two or more sense organs simultaneously, but we may stimulate "exchange" with other sensory areas when it reaches the brain.

Fifth, we may tie our stimulus to the previous conditioning of the other person. This is the most potent way to strengthen our stimulus. This can be a "multiplier" of the stimulus-strength as we will show in Chapter Three.

We Cannot Often "Raise Our Voice"

Even though the first and most obvious way to strengthen the stimulus is to make it strike the sense organ with greater impact, this is certainly not the best way, for several reasons.

If we raise our voice to make it hit the other person's ears harder, we may cause irritation. We may cause him to counter by raising his voice if he happens to have an objection. Shouting is not considered in good taste!

We can sometimes make things bigger—as when larger type is used to get attention in an advertisement. We can draw something big on a piece of paper and it gets more attention.

If we are to spank a child, we had best make sure that it is a "good spanking" so that he really feels it. In modern supermarkets they may use an invisible fan to blow the smell of delicious cooked foods across the aisles which the customers travel.

We may have to raise our voice now and then to get attention in a noisy room. This is a compensatory type of strengthening and does not cause another person to resent it. You have to shout to talk to someone in a boiler factory.

We Can Make It Travel Smoothly Along The Pathways

We can put our stimulus in a form, whether visual or spoken, which makes it travel the pathways to the mind in a smoother way. We can make it glide, not bump, along the pathways.

This involves certain techniques that precede the presentation of the stimulus. They are dealt with in detail in Chapters Four, Five, and Six. These are the techniques of presenting ideas in such a way that the other person is made receptive to them right at the start. There are similar techniques in Chapters Seven, Eight, Nine, and Ten which make it easier to oppose wrong ideas, wrong attitudes, or objections to our ideas.

Where Possible, Stimulate More Than One Sense Organ

Research shows that if a stimulus is presented simultaneously to two (or more) sense organs, it develops much more strength. Audio-visual training and television commercials are examples of this. Without going deeply into the scientific side of it, let me just say that such simultaneous presentation of your stimulus has more than twice the strength of presentations made to just one of the senses.

How can we do this? We may take a piece of paper and make a schematic diagram to illustrate the point we are making with our words, or we may go to a chart easel or blackboard. This hits the eyes and ears together. In selling we can get the person to "touch" the product or in selling a car, get him to "feel" the ride by taking him for a demonstration. As we point to a folder that extols the value of our product, we may read some of its beautiful phrases out loud. As we point to a balance sheet, we emphasize certain significant points with our words.

Remember: Try to think of ways to get the eyes and ears into the act at the same time! And if you can bring "touch" or "feel" into it, do that, too.

Get The Other Person's "Memory" Working For You

In our list, the fourth way to get the added effect of another sense organ at work is to make the person recall other sights, sounds, sensations, and feelings, perhaps tastes and smells. In this way, you get the person's memory or imagination to add a secondary, but important, stimulus.

The salesman of a car does this when he says: "When you feel the power of this engine out on the turnpike, you're going to be glad you bought it." Or he may say of the steering system, "When you see how this baby handles at seventy you're going to realize what I mean when I say that I'm 'selling peace of mind.' You'll know that the car is under control at all times just by the 'feel' of it."

Make it a habit to try to create favorable images with your words, evoke thoughts that add stimulation to other sense areas in the brain.

Most Important: Multiply The Power Of Your Stimulus!

When you reach Chapter 3, you're going to have a chance to study the most potent force of all in strengthening your stimulus. When a stimulus is linked to the prior conditioning of a person you deal with, its strength is multiplied. Yes, it is multiplied—not just increased as in addition. Interaction takes place, the kind of interaction that creates a powerful increment of motivation to respond favorably.

While we have used the words "prior conditioning" to describe the force to which you will link your stimulus, we can use another phrase—his "total experience." And, as in Chapter One, we can refer to it as "all of the things you have learned about him."

As we will see in Chapter Three, there are both "little" multipliers and "big" multipliers.

Let's See How These Ways To Strengthen Your Stimulus Work In a Real "Situation"

A "case history" in which all of these methods of making a

stimulus more powerful are used will help you to see how and what they do to get a response.

While names are changed, this is taken from a real life incident.

THE CASE OF THE STINGY GIVER

This has to do with the solicitation of a United Fund gift. A prominent business man, head of a sizable concern, had regularly returned his pledge card with a gift of only $25.00. He and/or his business should have been giving at least $250, in the opinion of those who knew his financial capability.

The fund drive committees for several years had tried to get him to increase his gift. His father, who started the business, had been dead for ten years, but had been one of the civic-minded men who had started the United Giving approach when the Community Chest had been created. Later it became the United Fund.

In talking over the problem with the Big Gifts Committee, we decided to get one of our best salesmen to work on his pledge. We knew that if we could get the head of the business to change his attitude, we could also get a chance to get a United Fund employee campaign started in his organization. A top notch former salesman, now a sales manager, agreed to attempt the task. We then planned the strategy to "change" this "stingy" giver.

In the following paragraphs I will use asterisks up to five in number to show how he strengthened his stimulus. The number of asterisks (from one through five) will show how he was strengthening his stimulus in terms of the numbers one through five shown in this chapter.

One other note: In earlier years, even coercion had been tried. One of his best customers had failed to change him.

This sales manager had only one small advantage: he had known him slightly in school.

Scene 1—The Secretary-Receptionist

With the pledge card, Bill Jones went to Charlie Roe's office.

The secretary said he was busy. Could she tell Mr. Roe who was calling? He raised his voice (so that Roe could hear—the door was open), "Tell him it's Bill Jones."*

Scene 2—The Opening

Soon Roe came to the door (after one of his own salesmen had come out). "Hi, Bill, haven't seen you for a long time."

"No, it's good to see you Chuck. Our paths haven't crossed since college." He got right to the point: "I came to see you about your United Fund pledge." He took out the pledge card and a United Fund folder.

The First Minor Objection

"Oh, well—just leave the card and I'll send it in."

"Well, I know that would be easier for both of us." (smoothing the pathway by conceding a point)** "But I promised the Senior Partners Committee that I would talk to you personally. Have you got the time to talk about it?"

The Second Minor Objection

"Oh, I suppose so. But if you're from the Big Gifts section, you might as well leave. I'm going to give what I gave last year."

"Well, I don't know exactly what you gave last year, but my goal is $250. That seems to be about right for you."

"That's ridiculous!"

Seeing And Hearing At The Same Time

Bill pulled out the folder, opened it up, held it across the desk. "Not when you realize that you're helping 27 different organizations, Chuck. Look at these children's and youth organizations." He read some of the names as he pointed to the UF beneficiaries.***

The First Major Objection

"Oh, I suppose those organizations and maybe the Red Cross are all right. But if I make a big gift a large part of it will go to

N00 (name of organization) and I wouldn't give them a nickel."

"Why don't you like the N00?"

"Let me tell you what happened ten years ago. . ." Roe recited a long-winded tale indicting the director of that organization for inefficiency and a personal affront.

"I remember him. I didn't particularly like him either. (smoothing the pathway by agreeing)** He's not connected with N00 anymore. The UF people didn't agree with some of his policies either.** Now N00 is much better managed. I was over there the other day and I wish you could see how they're handling things now. . ." Bill gave a description of the N00 current operations.****

The Second Major Objection

"O.K., so they've brainwashed you. But I'd want to see for myself that they've cleaned up before I started giving anything like $250."

"Well, I don't expect you to take my word for it. . .and it's not necessary that any of your gift go to N00. There's a space provided on the back where you can designate the UF beneficiaries that are to get your gift."**

The Third Major Objection—The "Put Off"

Chuck Roe was still trying to get out of the $250 gift. "Well, O.K. Leave the card and I'll think it over."

"Look, Chuck, I wouldn't mind doing that, but I don't want to go back to the Committee and tell them that we didn't get the job done today. We're getting close to the end of the drive and they want to button it up."

The "Magic" Multiplier

"Besides, one of the fellows on the Committee (it's someone else!) told me that your dad was one of the founders of the Community Chest. He was great for United Giving. Obviously, some of the men on the Committee were close to your dad. I hardly knew him—except people said that he had a heart that was as big as all outdoors when it came to helping others and building the community. I know that if your dad were alive, **he'd** fill that out for $250 and sign it!"***** (The "Multiplier")

Bill told me that there were tears in Chuck Roe's eyes as he picked up the card, filled it in for $300, and handed it back to Bill.

Bill Jones—An Expert In Dealing With People

In this remarkable incident, Bill Jones used every one of the five ways to strengthen his stimulus to get a response from Charles Roe. He succeeded where several others had failed. Why? He had learned how to develop power to deal with people. He used every means to strengthen his stimulus—to overcome objections and wrong ideas. He wound up by using a "multiplier" to close the sale!

The asterisks show you how Bill Jones strengthened his stimulus at each key point. In later chapters you will see how he used techniques described below to smooth the pathways to Charles Roe's consciousness and how he skillfully overcame Charles' objections.

You can learn to be as effective as Bill Jones.

To Get The Most Out Of This Chapter

To help you to remember that your stimulus must be strong enough to get a favorable action—not just lip service or token agreement—write down these five ways to make your stimulus stronger:

1. Increase its power or intensity.
2. Express it in such a way that it travels the pathways to the mind smoothly.
3. Appeal to more than one sense organ simultaneously.
4. Evoke images or recollections to bring additional areas of the mind (brain) into play.
5. Link your stimulus to the experience background (prior conditioning) of the other person.

Create a situation in which you can use each of these five ways to strengthen the power of a stimulus. Think of times when you might effectively raise your voice, for example. Think of ways to make your stimulus smoother, more able to travel the pathways to the mind smoothly. Think of ways to add a visual stimulus to an oral presentation or an oral stimulus to a visual presentation. Think of ways to add the sense of "touch" to your stimulus. Then think of ways in which you can evoke "images" in the mind of another person so that he "sees" what you are saying (in his mind, of course).

Finally, think of someone you know and see if you can find something in his prior conditioning to which you might link or tie your stimulus in order to get the "multiplier" effect.

Chapter Three

HOW TO
MULTIPLY YOUR POWER TO
INFLUENCE PEOPLE

We have learned in previous chapters that we can increase our power to influence others by sending strong messages along the pathways to the mind—the sense organs. We also learned that our influence is increased if we can present our stimulus to more than one sense organ.

We also learned that each human being has been *conditioned* by his past experience. If we can find out about his conditioning, especially as it relates to his need for security and his need to feel important, we can look for ways to link our presentation to his individual experience and background.

This *multiplies* your power to influence others.

How Much Does It Multiply?

When you have studied a person only briefly (as in the early part of your first conversation with him), the knowledge you have gained can at least double the power of your efforts to influence him. From the picture of a child on his desk or a plaque on the wall you may find some little reference point which will make him receptive. From the way he refers to his wife or from his comments on current affairs you may glean knowledge to which you can tie your efforts to influence him.

On the other hand, when you have had the opportunity to learn quite a bit about another person you may discover things about him that will increase your power by as much as tenfold! One young supervisor who attended one of my training courses coined the phrase "magic multiplier" to describe the power that he was able to develop by this means.

The big point to remember is: You will multiply your power to influence others if you relate your efforts to the experiences that have conditioned him in the past.

How To Use Some Of The "Little" Multipliers

Let's start out with some of the simple "little" multipliers that can almost always be discovered and used.

You see a diploma on the wall in a person's office. Later you introduce an idea by saying: "When you were in college. . ." You may even nod in the direction of the diploma.

You notice an American Legion or VFW pin in a man's lapel. Later you introduce an idea by saying: "It's like you learned when you were in the Service. . ."

You note that all the ash trays are empty. "Even though you don't smoke, you provide ash trays for your guests."

To a doctor you might say: "It's like the long hours you put in when you were an intern. . ."

To a lawyer: "When you were burning the midnight oil in law school, you probably wished. . ."

I know a salesman who always uses his pocket slide rule if he is calling on an engineer. But he never uses it when he is calling on a Sales Manager! He says that Sales Managers, generally, don't like "slide rule" people.

A salesman for mutual fund investment noticed the picture of my grandson on my back desk and inquired about it. Later he said: "If you save at this rate, you'll have $10,000 by the time he's ready for college."

On my back desk there are two large ceramic models of the famous chess set made by the French sculptor, Peter Ganine. A salesman noted them, and learned about my hobby—collecting chess sets. Later, to emphasize the importance of a point he was making he said: "This is like the queen on a chess board." (The queen is the most powerful piece in a chess game).

These little "multipliers" are only used casually or for purposes of illustration, yet they increase receptivity and thus build up the power of your presentation.

They may not accomplish "magic" as do some of the "multipliers" we will demonstrate later, but these "little" ones do accomplish three things:

1. They may provide you with an apt illustration or example that will make your point very clear.
2. They always make the other person feel more important because they build up his sense of personal worth.
3. They increase acceptance by the other person of you as a personality. The other person classifies you as a "good guy." You are alert to his likes, his needs.

Here's How The Major "Multipliers" Work

Beyond these "little" multipliers are the major ones that seem to accomplish "magic" under certain circumstances and conditions.

The major multipliers always have to do with a major phase of the *conditioning* of the person or persons you are striving to influence. They include:

1. His fundamental philosophy of life.
2. The people, activities, and possessions which make him feel important—increase his sense of personal worth.
3. A continuation of the behavior patterns which he has established as a "set" in his mind.

How A Supervisor Used Multipliers To Achieve "Magic"

The young supervisor who coined the phrase "magic multipliers" was in a management development group which met each week. After the session in which we discussed "multi-pliers," he stayed to discuss a particular problem he was facing in his department.

His problem was "spoiled work." In his department too much valuable metal went into the "salvage bin"—it was waste. Other parts had to be re-worked to meet standards. His cost, from week to week, ran from two to three times more than it should have been, based on averages.

Together we formulated a plan.

One week later he came back to the class enthusiastic and elated. He gave a "testimonial" to the others: "It works! That stuff we studied last week works like magic. It's like a 'magic multiplier.' "

How He Found The "Multipliers"

The other sixteen men in the training group were eager to learn exactly what he had done to cut down the "spoiled work." He unfolded his story:

He went to the Personnel Department and got the files on each of his machinists. He studied their backgrounds, especially their hobbies.

"If a guy was a golfer, I described salvage to him in terms of a bad shot—a lookup that he dug under or a topped shot that cost him a par. I told him that if he was doing his work right there wouldn't be any topped shots or lookups. . .no spoiled work.

"If he was a baseball player, I explained it to him in terms of an error. If he was a bowler, spoiled work became a 'gutter' ball. I explained spoiled work to each man in terms of his hobby."

Results were immediate and eventually the young supervisor reached a point at which his low salvage rate was the envy of every other supervisor.

Had he just stressed the importance of saving money for the company, he would have gotten some modest results. But the tie-in with the hobbies actually *multiplied* his power three or four times.

The "How" And The "Why" Of "Multipliers"

When you tie your effort to influence another person to an important aspect of his background, it does much more than just *add* to your power to influence him. The linkage produces *multiplication* because it makes *your* idea *his* idea. He *wants* to do what you want him to do.

The golfer hates to dub a shot. If you can make him transfer this dislike to his work, his errors will be reduced. A baseball player hates to make an error, a bridge player hates to go set, a chess player hates to lose his queen.

It works the same way on the positive side. In another situation a supervisor might relate work standards (the expected volume of output) to par in golf, to raising the team average in bowling, to improving the earned run average in baseball, etc.

The "how" involves finding out what makes this other person feel "ten feet tall." The "why" involves his own desire to improve and enhance his feeling of personal worth—his importance.

You Will Not Find It Difficult

The few minutes that this supervisor spent in studying the hobbies of his men produced a payoff that was well worth the small investment in time. It was not difficult for him.

It will not be difficult for you, once you decide to use "multipliers" to increase your power to deal with people.

When you have agreed with yourself that you are going to tie your efforts to the individual background of those you want to influence, you will find many ways to uncover "multipliers." Some of them will work like magic!

How To Look For "Multipliers"

If you have access to facts about hobbies, education, family, fraternal or civic connections, etc., it's easy to find "multipliers." Remember to look for and use such information when it is available.

For management and supervisory people, personnel records are obvious sources of such information.

For salesmen, city directories tell where a person works and sometimes where his spouse works. Directories of clubs, associations, and trade groups contain information about job titles and sometimes include education, hobbies, children, etc. Professional directories often contain biographical data. For people of some prominence, the "Who's Who" publications contain detailed biographical information. This includes regional "Who's Who In Commerce and Industry" publications as well as the national and world publications.

Moreover, you don't have to buy such publications—they are all in your local library!

There are four main sources of "multipliers":

1. Directories, publications, and personnel records.
2. Other people who know the person you want to influence.
3. Your own memory.
4. Asking questions and listening carefully.

Remember: "Stop And Think!"

One of the first steps in looking for a "multiplier" is "Stop—and think!" A little thought on your part may tell you quickly which of the four sources will be the most useful. Sometimes just a pause to reflect will bring things out of your own memory.

We underestimate the information stored in our own brains. A deliberate effort to recall what you already know about a person may produce the multiplier you're looking for. Some half-forgotten incident may uncover a hobby or avocation. The process may cause you to recall someone who knows the person better and can give you a "multiplier."

How To Use Other People To Find "Multipliers"

Sometimes when you use the "Stop and Think" approach, your first recollection will be the name or face of someone who knows that person better than you do.

Great salesmen talk to a person who knows their prospect

better than they do. A tool steel salesman whom I had known in school called me one day to ask me about a purchasing agent. He did not ask for information that was confidential. He asked questions like "Does he play golf?", "Does he have children?", etc. Companies who sell items of high value (such as industrial supplies) maintain files (sometimes called "customer profiles") in which they keep records of pertinent information about the responsible person who must "sign the order."

This brings to mind an example of how a "magic multiplier" was discovered by asking a few simple questions of a person who knew the other person better.

THE CASE OF THE GAMBLING PROSPECT

During a training session for a Frigidaire wholesaler, the General Manager, Roy Wood, gave a good example of how he had used a "multiplier" to turn a lost sale into a sale.

A wealthy prospect in a nearby city was completing a large 12-room house and planned a housewarming to which every important person in town would be invited. He had plans to install a 12-cubic-foot refrigerator in the spacious kitchen. It was in the summer of 1927 and that was the largest refrigerator made in those days.

The prospect had been very cagey: He had asked for the price and the specification sheets for Frigidaire. No sales presentation was allowed. "When the dealer called me," Roy said, "the sale was lost. The man had said he was going to buy a Norseman* because it was a hundred dollars cheaper—$595 against our $695. The dealer was fit to be tied."

Roy agreed to drive down and try to save the sale. He told the dealer to make an appointment for 9:00 the next morning and said that he would meet with the dealer at 8:00.

Finding The "Magic Multiplier"

When Roy arrived, he took the dealer out for coffee. They

---

*Name has been changed

spent most of the hour discussing the prospect. The wealthy prospect had made his money in oil. He also enjoyed gambling and usually won. He was a heavy better on sports, including baseball. He followed sports very closely. Roy said: "There it was—the thing you call a 'multiplier.' "

"Two Strikes" On Roy Wood

"I had two strikes on me when we opened the conversation," said Roy. "When I shook hands with this guy he said, 'Glad to meet the hot shot from Wichita who's going to try to talk me out of throwing away a hundred bucks just to pay for the Frigidaire name.' "

After Roy was seated across the desk the prospect spoke up aggressively. "Now you tell me what's wrong with a Norseman. I've looked at the specifications and can't see any difference."

Roy said: "I don't know of anything that's wrong with a Norseman. By the way, Charlie tells me that you follow sports closely. How did the Yankees come out yesterday?"

"Huh! They murdered the White Sox."

"Where do they play today?"

"Cleveland—three game series on the way home."

Roy leaned across the desk. "I'll bet you ten dollars, even money, that the Yankees beat the Indians today."

The prospect snorted. "What do you take me for? That's not an even money bet! The Yanks win two out of three games they play."

Roy came right back. "That's right. The Yankees have the best record in baseball. Frigidaire has the same kind of record in refrigeration. . .eleven years of proven service on the hottest days a Kansas summer can bring.

"When you asked me what was wrong with a Norseman, I said I didn't know. I was telling the truth. Norseman just started two years ago. They don't have a record like Frigidaire, and it will take more than just one summer to see if they can match us."

The "Clincher"

"Like any smart gambler you would not take an even money

bet against the Yankees. The odds are against their losing.

"What we're suggesting is that you use the same logic in buying a refrigerator. Bet on a proven winner instead of an unknown. If you put your money on Frigidaire—the Yankees of the refrigeration business—you only have to pay odds of seven to six, in round numbers."

A "Home Run" Instead Of A Third Strike

The millionaire hesitated a moment, pensively, then turned to the dealer. "You know, Charlie, he's right. Those aren't bad odds if you want to be sure you get a dependable machine. Order me that twelve-footer and be sure it gets here before Labor Day. That's when we'll have our housewarming."

The "multiplier" worked.

With two strikes on him, Roy Wood hit a home run because he had found a "multiplier."

The Gambler's Way Of Life

Roy Wood's "multiplier" was tied into the way of life of the wealthy prospect. Shrewd, he resented paying $100 additional for a refrigerator that appeared to him to be the same in its specifications. That, to him, would reduce his sense of personal worth. But the minute that that $100 was expressed in terms of gambling odds, short odds at that, coupled with the importance that would be tied to displaying the product with the best record in his new home, he changed immediately. Roy Wood had tied the refrigerator, its quality, and its price to a part of the prospect's way of life. Just a few minutes over a cup of coffee had given him his "magic multipler."

THE CASE OF THE UNSAFE PRESS OPERATOR

Jim, a press operator in the Stamping Department of The Coleman Company of Wichita, was violating safety rules. In order to run his press faster, he was tying back one of the dual controls. In this way he could feed material with his left hand, pull the right-hand control with his right hand. He thought this increased his production and his bonus earnings. It also meant that the press might amputate his left hand or arm!

Everything, up to and including the threat of being discharged, had been done to try to get him to stop.

We Studied Jim

In a conference with Jim's foreman, the Safety Engineer, and the Personnel Director, we looked over Jim's personnel file. He played on an amateur baseball team, a regular first baseman and relief pitcher. More important, the record showed that he and his wife had a young son, now twenty-one months old.

When I asked the foreman about the son, the foreman laughed. "Jim is just crazy about that kid. Takes a new snapshot of him every month or so. Carries it in his wallet. Ask how the kid is and the picture comes out. Then he takes about ten minutes telling you about him. Now he's got a picture of the kid throwing a ball. You'd think he was a young Dizzy Dean."

There it was—the "multiplier."

How The Safety Engineer Used The "Multiplier"

It was hard to catch Jim in his unsafe practice because he used a bent coat hanger to hold the control. He could pull it off quickly if he saw the foreman coming. So it was decided that the Safety Engineer would surprise him by coming in a side door. He did this the next morning. "How's that boy of yours, Jim?"

"You oughta see that kid." Out came the wallet and a picture of the little boy throwing a ball.

The Safety Engineer took the wallet from Jim, removed the picture. Then he mounted it with Scotch tape right next to the left-hand trip lever. "Look, Jim, while you don't seem to care about losing some fingers or your hand or half of your arm, that boy does. He cares. He wants a Daddy that has two good hands and arms and can play ball with him—teach him how to throw a curve." He reached up and took the bent coat hanger, threw it in the trash. "Everytime you think about tying that control, that picture ought to remind you how that son of yours would feel about it. He wouldn't want you to take that risk."

It Was "Like Magic"

The "multiplier" worked "like magic." Jim's foreman and his co-workers were amazed to see that the picture stayed where the Safety Engineer had put it. Jim became an apostle of safety. Everything else had failed, but the boy and his picture succeeded in changing Jim. The boy was the most important thing in Jim's life, a "magic multiplier."

Sometimes You "Play It By Ear"

In both of these cases, the "multiplier" was discovered in advance—either by talking to a person who knew or by studying records or both. When you don't have access to advance information you "play it by ear." You ask leading questions and listen carefully for a clue to find a "multiplier." Many salesmen do this. They find "multipliers" by the way they question the prospect in the early stages of the interview.

Let's look at a case which illustrates this technique.

THE CASE OF THE "UPSIDE DOWN" WASHER SALES

This case history shows how Harold, an appliance salesman, closed two automatic washer sales on the same day. The buying motives were exactly opposite—"upside down."

The Woman Who Washed Her Own "Fine Things"

Just before noon, a well-dressed woman stopped to look at the Frigidaire washer which was churning bright-colored pieces of cloth near the aisle of this department store. Harold stepped over, introduced himself, got her name, then asked "What kind of washer do you have, Mrs. Bond?"

"I don't have a washer. No need for one. There's just my husband and I and we both work. Our laundry goes out, except for my own *fine things.* I wash them by hand—wouldn't want them in a washer. Anyway, I was just coming in to pay my bill."

Harold Had Found A "Multiplier"

Mrs. Bond wanted a washer that was so gentle that it would not hurt her "fine things." Harold agreed with her that most washers would tend to abrade fine silks and nylons. . .except he called them her "fine things," feeding back her own words. Then he showed her how the Frigidaire washer simply flushed water through the clothing, did not rub, tumble, or hold it around an impeller. He proved all of this with a demonstration. "And in addition to being gentler on your fine things—gentler than even hand-washing could be—you can do all of your bedding and your husband's underclothing—anything that doesn't need ironing."

Mrs. Bond bought the washer—because it would be kind to her "fine things"—the "multiplier" that Harold discovered by his early questioning.

Harold's Question: "What Kind Of Washer?"

Harold always asked the same question: "What kind of washer do you have?" This gave him the information he needed to link his presentation to the prospect's background. Even Mrs. Bond, who had no washer, felt compelled to tell him why she had none—thereby uncovering the "multiplier," the "fine things."

But This Woman Wanted A Different Kind Of Washer

Later that same day, a short plump woman came hurrying up to the washer display. Harold asked the same question: "What kind of washer do you have?"

"That's the trouble. Up till yesterday I had an old Magic-Wash*. But the motor burned out and my husband says it

---

*Name has been changed

would cost more to fix it than it's worth." She went on to say that her husband had come home from work and was sitting with their three pre-school boys while she shopped. She intended to look at three brands.

Harold also learned that her husband was a machinist whose work clothes picked up a lot of oil and dirt.

Harold Showed How His Washer Removed Heavy Soil

Harold mentioned that he had two small boys. "Mary, my wife, says she'd rather have plenty of clean clothes for the boys than to scold them about getting dirty." Mrs. Johnson beamed her approval.

Then he took a large piece of white denim, stained it with dirty crankcase oil, put it in the washer. It came out spotless, but while the washer was working he went into its features in detail. He did not mention how gently it would handle silks and nylons—oh, no!

Mrs. Johnson and her husband came back that evening and bought the washer. She did not "shop" the other two brands that she had mentioned earlier.

Magic "Multipliers"—But Upside Down!

Mrs. Bond wanted a gentle washer for her "fine things." Mrs. Johnson wanted a hard-working washer that would remove heavy soil. They bought the same washer for opposite reasons!

He learned about those reasons from skillful questioning. Then he made the most of the opposing buying motives. He didn't mention to Mrs. Johnson how gentle his washer was, nor to Mrs. Bond about how it would remove heavy soil. That would have placed his "multiplier" in jeopardy!

A Note Of Warning:

And these two cases point up a danger that is found in some sales training which stresses touching on all the product features: It may lose sales! If you stick to the product features that tie into the "multiplier" you're on safe ground.

Build Habits That Force You To Study People

Regardless of which method or combination of methods you use to find "multipliers," the first step is to get into the habit. Force yourself to think: "What is different or unusual about this person?" As you open a conversation with someone that you know little or nothing about, think of questions that will draw him out.

Force yourself to take note of differences in advance of an interview. If you're waiting in an outer office, look at the pictures, talk to the receptionist. After you are inside the office, keep your eyes open. What kind of pictures or decorations are on the wall? Note if there are framed diplomas, awards, etc. These give strong clues as to what satisfies this person's need for a feeling of personal worth.

How To Develop Skill In Questioning

We made a point of the fact that Harold, the automatic washer salesman, always started his interview with, "What kind of washer do you have?" This cannot be answered "Yes" or "No", as we pointed out. It is the kind of question which a woman usually answers by describing her home situation with relation to laundry.

Skill in asking questions starts from learning to ask questions that cannot be answered with a word or two. This involves the use of the interrogative pronouns—who? what? where? when? and how?

Who?

The answer to this question may be very revealing. It may tell a salesman who is influencing the sale—who suggested it, who directed him to your place of business. If I can learn from a person who inquires about our company who it was that referred him to us, I am well on the way to discovering a "multiplier." At least I will learn who to thank for the referral! Salesmen, foremen, supervisors, executives are always interested in knowing "who" exerts an influence over the person they want to influence.

What? And Which?

"What" and "which" cannot be answered with a "yes" or a "no." "What" permits a person to expand and tell you much more than is evident from the apparent purpose of the question. Sometimes "which" is even better because it narrows down choices. Alternatives expressed in advance help you to see how the person thinks.

Where?

The car salesman may ask "Where do you do most of your driving?" This will give him a wealth of information. "Where did you spend your vacation?" "Where do you live?" There are things to be learned about a person if he expands on his answer to a "where?" question.

When?

The element of time—the answer to "when"—does not often lead to multipliers, but sometimes it proves useful. If a car salesman has not seen the car the prospect is driving, this word will tell him how old it is, for example.

How?

This is the most useful of the interrogatives. It demands more in the form of information than any of the others.

"How long have you been driving your (present car)?" is better than "when did you buy it?" because it calls for an answer that evokes recollection. The individual thinks back to how many months he has had it and this may cause him to recall and mention incidents that are helpful to the car salesman in finding a "magic multiplier."

Supervisors make good use of this. When working with a colleague or subordinate they can literally see how the person thinks when he responds to the question: "How are we going to solve this problem?"

How To Use Empathy To Multiply Your Influence

Those who want to build up their power to influence people need to develop what psychologists call "empathy." This is the ability to "put yourself in the other person's shoes." Alertness to the feelings of others helps to find the "multipliers" and to have others ready to accept your influence.

The dictionary defines empathy as "the projection of one's own consciousness into another being."

Some persons, usually more sensitive than the average person, seem to have been born with a natural tendency to employ empathy in dealing with people. This is a liability if it makes them reluctant to strive to get others to do things they want them to do.

However, one does not have to be sensitive or supersensitive to develop empathy; it can be developed as a "skill." Once you have committed yourself to the idea that you want to learn more about those you wish to influence, you will find it easy to achieve empathy. This commitment works for almost any type of personality, from the super-sensitive person to the rough-and-tumble hardy personality.

Develop Empathy Through Keen Observation

Empathy is not sympathy. The sensitive person feels sorry for the other person and does not want to offend him. He feels that he should handle people with the same "soft gloves" that he wants others to use in handling him. Thus over-sensitive people are super-cautious.

All of us should be cautious in handling sensitive people. But all people are not extremely sensitive. They range from the highly sensitive to the very insensitive. And in-between you'll find people who are really more sensitive than others, but who have put on a hard shell of apparent ruggedness to conceal (or protect) their sensitivity.

If you are keenly observant, the other person will tell you how he wants to be treated. He won't tell you in so many words, but he will tell you by gesture and expression.

Watch for signs of approval or disapproval. Watch for smiles and frowns. Listen for key words and phrases that tell you more about the kind of person you're dealing with!

To Get The Most Out Of This Chapter

1. Take some person you know fairly well and make notes about him. This could be your boss, a fellow worker, a social acquaintance. After making the notes see if you can write down a "multiplier."
2. Go through the same process for someone very close to you, your husband or wife, your children.
3. Now follow the same process for someone you know only slightly. After you have put down what you know about him (her) add to your notes (1) Who can I talk to who knows him better than I? (2) What records could I study to get more information about him?
4. The next time you meet a person whom you do not know at all, test out your questioning technique. Ask questions which will draw him out. Let him talk. Listen carefully. Then, when you get alone, make notes about what he said. See if you can find a "multiplier" in those notes.

CHECK LIST TO FIND "MULTIPLIERS"

Ways To Find Them In Advance Of An Interview

1. Records
   a. Personnel Records (for supervisors, executives)
   b. Service Records (salesmen)
   c. City Directories
   d. Biographical Directories (Who's Who, etc.)
   e. Professional Directories and Membership Lists
   f. Credit Records and Dun and Bradstreet reports

2. Inquiry—Who Knows Him Better Than I?
   a. Friends and acquaintances
   b. Employer
   c. Professional associates
   d. Social conversation (Do you know so-an-so?)

3. Recollection and Recall—What Do I Know About Him?
   a. Hobbies
   b. Politics
   c. Religion
   d. Education
   e. Organizations he belongs to—fraternal, civic, business
   f. Children—ages and sex
   g. Wife or husband—hobbies, organizations, etc.

Ways To Find Them "On The Spot" (During Or Just Preceding Your Presentation)

1. Surroundings
   a. Pictures or photographs
   b. Desk ornaments or gadgets
   c. Clothing
   d. Fraternal or club emblems or buttons
   e. Books or magazines
   f. Evidences of hobbies or avocations
   g. Awards, diplomas, honors
   h. Arrangement of furniture

2. Asking Questions
   a. About surroundings
   b. Do you know? (a mutual acquaintance)
   c. Who-What-Which-When-Where-How?
   d. Current events

3. Observing Reactions
   a. What makes him smile?
   b. Any evidence of displeasure?
   c. Any evidence of impatience?

4. Careful Listening
   a. What does he mean? (Not just what does he say?)

b. Listen for remembering (repeat important things the person says to "set" them in your mind)

Chapter Four

HOW TO DEVELOP POWER
IN PRESENTING
YOUR IDEAS TO OTHERS

A very dependable source of motivation is the need for a feeling of personal worth (Chapter One). It is always present in all of us. The more powerful "multipliers" of Chapter Three were tied closely to the personal worth of the person influenced—the hobbies of the machinists, the "good gamble" for the wealthy gambler, the fine lingerie of the woman who didn't need a washer, the desire to provide plenty of clean clothes for the other washer buyer, the love for the twenty-one-month-old baby boy by the press operator.

In each of these cases, the discovery of a major or minor factor contributing to the personal worth of the person being influenced multiplied the force of the presentation. In this chapter and the two which follow, we will show how personal worth is related to each idea you present to another person.

Expect Resistance To Your Ideas—Unless ...

When you present your idea to another person he usually has

a natural tendency to resist accepting it. It is your idea, not his. If he accepts it without resistance, he is admitting that you thought of it first, that you have better ideas than he, or that he "missed" the idea in his approach to a problem or situation.

If he accepts your idea without resistance he feels a loss of personal worth. It may be only slight, but it is there.

Let's face it: No matter how good our ideas are, they are going to have hard sledding to get acceptance. Unless . . .

You Can Learn How To Protect The Other Person's Personal Worth

Yes, the natural resistance to your ideas can be removed or reduced if you present them in a way that protects the personal worth of the other person. There are specific techniques which accomplish this end. Summed up, these techniques involve:

1. Presenting the idea in such a way that accepting it will add to his personal worth.
2. Presenting the idea in a way that assures that his personal worth will not be *reduced* by accepting it.

Don't Be Misled By A "Show" Of Acceptance

Some persons, usually well-educated or possessed of much natural empathy, conceal their resistance to the ideas of others. They make a "show" of acceptance in order to appear open-minded and receptive. Later, when the "chips are down" you find that they didn't really accept the idea. They said they would do something and then didn't do it. They reached the closing point in the sale and then said, "I'll think it over." Remember: Your idea has not been accepted until some action has resulted. You have not *influenced* another person until you have effected a change in his behavior in the direction that you wanted him to change.

If you present your idea with careful regard and attention to his need for a feeling of personal worth, you don't have to concern yourself about follow-through on his part.

The Way To Avoid Argument

Unless you link your idea to his Personal Worth or present it in such a way that it doesn't reduce it, you may find yourself with an argument on your hands.

The flat, blunt, "MY idea" approach causes the other person to search his mind for reasons to prove your idea is not as good as you think it is. It inspires such responses as "It won't work out in practice," "We've tried that before," "I thought of that, but gave it up because. . ." Failure to use proper techniques causes arguments. It increases resistance.

First Step: Don't Seek "Credit" For Your Ideas

In working with young people, especially supervisors and staff people in management, I frequently find them saying: "If I follow this method, use these techniques, I won't get 'credit' from other people for my ideas." They sometimes say: "If I convince the boss that it's HIS idea, he'll take the credit for it."

My first reply to such expressions of doubt comes from practical experience. First, normal, well-adjusted people are not trying to "steal" ideas. Second, when the boss accepts an idea that will produce profit or improve operations, he has a right to some credit for having accepted it. Experience indicates that the person who puts over his idea gets credit for it ultimately.

The first step in becoming effective in influencing others is to forget about "credit" for your ideas. Forcing another person to admit that it was your idea and not his puts an insurmountable barrier in the path of your idea. You must develop the attitude of the good "team" man—the most important thing is to put the idea over!

This is never a problem to the great salesman. He could care less about getting "credit" from the customer for a good idea. He is primarily interested in completing the sale! He gets his "credit" from the commission, the winning of the sales contest, etc.

You should develop the attitude that getting people to do what you want them to do is your reward. Dwight Eisenhower defined the "art of leadership" as "getting people to do what *you* want them to do because *they* want to do it." You should be primarily ₁concerned with the end result. You are not going to achieve the end result unless "*they* want to do what you want them to."

Experts Recognize These Techniques

In the techniques which we will describe in this chapter and the two that are to follow, you will see many that you have used. When I am working with a group of supervisors that have had experience, they always say: "I've used about half of those techniques." They learned them by trial-and-error. Some seasoned salesmen will tell me that they have used two-thirds of the techniques described in this and the following chapters.

However, both salesmen and supervisors, people who make their living by influencing others, see the value of the other techniques that they had not discovered. Experts in dealing with people have given me their reactions to these techniques.

A salesman with twenty years of successful experience said: "I checked off those techniques and found I had used all but five of the 19. I can sure think of times when I could have used those other five!"

A supervisor said: "With this kind of a check list, I can refer to it and pick out techniques which are especially suited to different situations."

How You Develop "Change Of Pace"

The big advantage in these techniques lies in the diversity they provide for you. A salesman called it "change of pace."

When you look at these techniques you will come upon one which will prompt you to say: "I've used that one many times!" You have probably overworked that technique.

When you study *all* of the techniques, you'll achieve diversity, change of pace. You won't sound like a "broken record."

You Want To Be Like A Major League Pitcher

While every pitcher has one or two pitches that he favors, he does not become seasoned and enjoy a great year until he has several different pitches. If he can use only the fast ball or the change-up, some hitters are going to hit him hard. When he adds one or more curves, a floater or a screw ball, he increases his effectiveness.

So it is with the techniques we are offering you. They are all useful. They permit you to proceed through several phases of a presentation without losing diversity and freshness.

Three Types Of Techniques

We will provide you with 19 different ways to present your ideas to others. All of them relate to the idea we expressed at the start of this chapter: (1) They make him feel that accepting the idea will build up his personal worth, or (2) They prevent the presentation from reducing his sense of personal worth.

The 19 Techniques fall into three natural groups:

1. Techniques which make the other person feel the idea is his own.
2. Techniques which build up or protect his personal worth as a preface to presenting the idea.
3. Techniques which make him feel he will *lose* personal worth if he does *not* accept the idea.

We will cover group 1 in this chapter.

PRESENTING THE IDEA IN SUCH A WAY THAT THE OTHER PERSON FEELS THAT IT IS HIS

There are eight ways to present an idea in such a way that the other person feels that it is his own.

However, it is easier to remember them if we separate them into three groups based on these common characteristics:

A. Three of the techniques are based on *assuming* that the other person has accepted the idea.

A-1   Offer him a choice which assumes that he has accepted the idea.

A-2   Use a word such as "after," "when," or "as," which assumes he will accept it.

A-3   *Remind* him of the idea as if he already knew it and had accepted it.

R. Two others are classified as "R" techniques because they *relate* the idea to his previous behavior or expressed ideas.

R-1   Show that the idea follows along with his previous behavior or expressed idea.

R-2   Present the idea as if something he had said suggested it.

E. Three techniques are classified as "E" techniques because they involve getting him to *"express"* the idea himself.

E-1   Present a series of facts pointing toward our idea and let him draw the conclusion.

E-2   Ask a question, the answer to which is our idea.

E-3   Discuss a general situation touching or relating to the idea until the other person expresses it.

These three classifications may be easier to remember if you note that they spell the word "ARE." These *ARE* the best techniques to get full acceptance of your ideas.

Now let's look at each technique more closely and show examples of how they work in real life situations.

"A" TECHNIQUES—ASSUMING ACCEPTANCE

A-1   Offer A Choice Which Assumes Acceptance

This is one of the oldest and most-used techniques as a means to close a sale. Clerks are trained to use it. Salesmen of automobiles and specialties use it. Supervisors use it to "nail down" the acceptance of the idea.

Part of its merit lies in the fact that the making of the choice results in an expression, a statement by the other person. Thus it has some of the elements of the "E" techniques.

The Sales Situation

The sales clerk says, "Will you take it with you or shall we send it out?" Either choice means the sale is closed. The same is true of the high-fashion salesgirl who says: "Do you prefer the blue or the aqua model?"

The technique is especially useful to the salesman with a wide assortment of models and features. Use of this technique coupled with close observation of the prospect may let him know when to use a similar question for a "closer."

The Supervisory Situation

One of the problems faced by the supervisor is the need to get commitment on an idea involving a program expected of subordinates. The fact that he offers some choice increases motivation and acceptance, yet "nails down" the acceptance so that it can't be delayed or forgotten. If such a supervisor has a new method or system to "sell" he may finalize it by saying: "Can we start this tomorrow or do we need another day?"

The Personal or Home Situation

A young executive, noting an invitation to an important party in the household mail, but hoping to stave off the cost of a new dress, may say to his wife: "Are you going to wear your figured dress or the blue satin to the party? They both look swell on you."

A mother might say to a bath-resistant child: "Would you rather take your bath before you watch 'Bonanza' or afterward?"

With a little ingenuity and application you will find many ways to offer choices which will gain acceptance of your idea. The other person will feel that it was his idea all the time!

A-2 Use A Word Which Assumes Acceptance

If you express your idea after an introduction which uses a word such as "After," "When" or "As" the final effect on the other person is that it is his idea. He will carry it out in the

future. The introductory phrases are, "After you have. . .,"
"When you try. . .," or "When you see. . ." and "As you follow
through on this. . .," etc.

Important: Never use the word "If." It has two weaknesses.
It reaffirms the state of indecision or non-acceptance and it may
imply a threat if the emphasis is wrong. The implication of a
threat may cause the person to "bow his neck" and start
resistance that cannot be stopped.

The Supervisory Situation

An industrial trainer, after demonstrating an improved way
of doing the job, can use this technique effectively: "When you
have done this for two or three days, you'll find that you
produce just as much, but are less tired when you go home."

Introducing a new supervisor, especially one who comes from
"outside" the company, can be done in this way: "After you
have worked with Charlie awhile, you'll see how he can find
short-cuts and easier ways to do your work."

The Sales Situation

The salesman can use this technique to evoke an image of
future ownership in the prospect's mind. "When you have this
300-horsepower engine out on the turnpike, you'll appreciate
its power and smoothness at high speeds."

The high-fashion sales girl might say: "I can see you at the
next big party with all eyes looking at you in this dress."

The Personal or Home Situation

Having trouble getting your child to do his homework? Try:
"After you have finished your homework you can watch TV for
30 minutes before bedtime."

You'd like to get your "crowd" to give up an expensive trip
to a night club: "After we look at 'Western World' on TV, let's
play penny ante for awhile."

Your wife might respond if you said: "After I saw you in

that blue satin, I said to myself, 'I hope she doesn't hang it up and forget it.' "

A-3   We "Remind" Him Of The Idea

If we "remind" a person about an idea, he feels it was his idea. However, in conducting training sessions, I find that some individuals are reluctant to try this technique for fear that the other person may say: "I don't remember that!" Actually this seldom happens and even when it does, there is no resentment. The idea is still accepted because personal worth was protected.

The Sales Situation

An automobile salesman may say: "You'll remember that the most dangerous period in high speed driving is the period when you're passing another car. The higher horsepower engine cuts down passing time."

The air conditioning salesman could say: "Let me remind you that humidity has as much to do with personal comfort as temperature. On a hot day, our air conditioner performs in this way . . ."

In talking to hundreds of salesmen, I have never heard of one instance in which a customer challenged such "reminders" even when the information was technical!

The Supervisory Situation

If you are talking to an engineer, you can say: "You will remember from calculus that data of this type tends to group itself in this way . . . "

The supervisor says to the machine operator: "When you studied about preventive maintenance they told you. . ."

The Personal and Home Situation

A parent might say: "Remember that your eyes get tired when you watch television, so do your homework before you watch TV."

And in talking to your social "crowd" to get them to stay home Saturday night: "Remember how much fun we had the night we played penny ante?"

"R" TECHNIQUES WHICH RELATE YOUR IDEA TO HIM

R-1   Show That The Idea Follows Along With His Previous Behavior Or Expressed Idea

If you know about a person's previous behavioral habits or practices or if you have heard him express a position that comes close to it, linking your idea to that behavior or to his idea will gain better acceptance for you.

This (in contrast to R-2 which follows) covers a broad spectrum. It may *relate* (R) to his station in life, his politics or religion or any known pattern of behavior that "fits" your need. It may *relate* to something he has said in the past or earlier in the interview. It is different from R-2 because R-2 involves the thought that he *suggested* the idea by something he said. By contrast, R-1 involves a continuation of his behavior or philosophy.

The Sales Situation

Salesmen use this technique when dealing with "repeat" customers. "You've been a Chevy owner for years and you know how we have continued to improve our products. This year there are several new things." Almost the same conversation might be used for a known "repeat" user of any product.

It was this technique, of course, that Roy Wood used in the Case of The Gambling Prospect. He established the prospect's "pattern" of life and then tied his idea to the calculation of gambling odds.

A sales engineer can use this when his prospect is either an engineer or accountant. "As an engineer you want exact data and that's why these records on the field-testing of our products are important to you."

The Supervisory Situation

The technique is useful, as we saw in the case of the supervisor who was striving to cut down spoiled work, where we can find out about the person's behavior from hobbies or other background facts. Good work can be *related* to anything from good golf to good chess playing. It can also be related to expressed goals and general aims.

A supervisor might say: "When you came to work on that first day six months ago you told me that you felt this was your career—this company. Now one important thing you need to learn about our operations is. . ."

A crew chief could say: "Several times at coffee breaks I've heard you talk about the importance of team effort. If you think of our crew as a 'team,' you'll see how important this new method can be."

The Personal and Home Situation

In social and home situations the opportunities to use this are almost limitless. People express their philosophies to their families and their close friends. Often they can be *related* to ideas that you want to put across.

A father might say to his son: "Last summer you told me that the Little League coach gave you some extra practice to help you get control with your fast ball. Each new thing that we undertake may require some extra effort at the start. That's the way it is with algebra."

Wife to husband: "You've always mentioned how much you enjoy meeting new people at your civic club. I think you'd enjoy meeting the people I know at PTA."

R-2 Present The Idea As If Something He Had Said Suggested It

In this technique the connection between what the other person said and the fact that it "suggested" the idea may be tied very closely or it may be quite "thin". Regardless of whether the connection is close or "thin," it still offers opportunity to make him feel that it was his idea.

The Sales Situation

Alert salesmen are continually on the watch for statements of prospects that "suggest" presentation of product features.

A car salesman might say: "You mentioned you were in the insurance business. That made me think of the fact that some of our new features are like insurance for the car owner."

The high-fashion salesgirl might say: "I noticed that you were looking at the label in that dress and that brought to mind the fact that all the garments in this department are exclusives. You won't see anyone wearing one like them."

This one (above) does not involve something the prospect said, but something she did. An act may be the key to the "suggestion" as well as a statement.

The Supervisory Situation

A supervisor, trying to cut down on the cost of waste in his department might say: "You were talking about the high cost of living at the coffee break. You know, the company is facing the same problem. Costs are going up faster than business is increasing. As a result we're watching every expense to see if we can bring it down. Take salvage, for example."

A methods analyst or engineer might say to an operator: "When you mentioned how tired you were after a day's work, I though of how you handle your right arm in this operation. When we took moving pictures of you at your machine, we found that you move your right arm much too far."

The Personal or Home Situation

A wife might say: "You mentioned that you had a big insurance premium coming on the first of the month. That made me think that if I bought a new dress for the Johnsons' party after the 28th of the month, it wouldn't be on our bill until a month later. Then you'd be out of the woods on the insurance premium." Very clever.

A father might say: "When you mentioned what the coach said about practice, it made me realize that there's a reason for those heavy problem assignments in this first part of your algebra course."

Now let's turn to the "E" techniques.

"E" TECHNIQUES—HE WILL "EXPRESS" YOUR IDEA

E-1   Present A Series Of Facts Pointing Toward Your Idea So That He Will Express It As A Conclusion

Most people are gratified or pleased when they can anticipate a conclusion derived from a series of facts. As a result they are quick to express such a conclusion.

At this point, the individual who presents the series of facts has only to agree with the conclusion. "You're right."

Historians tell us that this was Benjamin Franklin's favorite tool for persuasion. He used it to achieve a major contribution to the winning of the Revolutionary War.

The Federated Colonies, at war with England, were sorely in need of money to bolster their weak financial position which was preventing the prosecution of the war with full vigor. Ben Franklin was sent to France to try to arrange a loan for the Colonies and was granted an appearance before the court of King Louis.

Didn't Ask For Money

Did Ben come right out and ask for money? No. With his skill in the use of this technique he simply presented an array of facts. The British were a threat to France. This threat would be reduced if England had to divert more men and money to fight the American Revolution. England was already so hard put for men that she had "hired" 30,000 Hessian mercenaries from Germany. The Colonists were having trouble paying their troops and buying supplies. A series of related facts had been presented by Franklin.

After the presentation, the King counselled with his advisors and offered a treaty—the Treaty of 1777. It has been said that this treaty included the offer of a loan that was three times the amount that Franklin would have dared to ask for! In addition, his presentation aroused the interest of the Marquis de Lafayette, who not only offered his trained troops, but came to America to give them leadership. What a selling job by Ben Franklin!

The King of France and the Marquis de Lafayette felt that it was *their* idea. Since it was *their* idea, they were motivated to the maximum. Franklin presented the facts. They drew the conclusion.

You Ask: "But How Can I Do It?"

You may ask: "How can I make a presentation like this in an informal discussion? Franklin had three months on a boat to plan his presentation in detail. No wonder he could impress the court of France!"

A rather simple example could be shown from the situation described earlier (R-2) concerning the upcoming party at the Johnsons' and the dress.

Her Husband Could Pull A "Ben Franklin"

Anticipating a plea for a new dress to go to the Johnsons' party, the husband might say: "You know honey I've got that big life insurance premium that hits me next month. And then in August, we'll have to get the three kids outfitted for school and pay for Johnny's summer camp."

His wife may be disappointed, but she's going to save and enhance her personal worth. She's the BIG person who makes it HER idea: "Well, I guess I had better not plan to get a new dress for the Johnsons' party."

The Sales Situation

A salesman knows that the prospect's car is three years old. He knows that it is in good condition, so he has to emphasize things that are new in the past three years. He quickly recaps in his mind the new things that are standard. He says: "A lot of new things have come along in the past three model years. Seat belts are standard, headlights are protected against daytime hazards, the new locks and ignition switches protect against theft, doors have new safety features. . .there's a lot of built-in safety in the new cars." It is logical for the prospect to say: "Yeah, I know. There are none of those things on the car I'm driving."

The Supervisory Situation

A supervisor wants to impress a workman with the importance of increasing his output. He builds up by saying: "At our foreman's meeting Monday morning, the Plant Superintendent told us how costs are going up. The Sales Department showed us the new low priced Japanese products that are competing with ours. The Japanese have lower labor costs and higher productivity per worker."

The workman comes back: "It looks like we've got to produce more or we'll ALL be out of a job."

Suppose The Other Person Doesn't Reach The Conclusion?

If the other person does not see or does not express the conclusion, you can go ahead and draw the conclusion for him. It is not quite as effective as if he actually expressed it, but it is still more effective than if you had not presented the series of facts which make your conclusion logical. You would simply say: "So you can see why. . ." or, "That's why it's logical to. . ."

With a little thought you'll find plenty of uses for this technique. You'll be pleasantly surprised at how often the other person proudly draws the conclusion. It's his idea!

E-2   Ask a Question, The Answer To Which Expresses Your Idea

Skill in questioning involves skill in getting the other person to think about what you want him to think about. A question can often cause a person to express the idea you want him to have.

The use of the interrogatives mentioned in Chapter Three bears heavily on success in using this technique. The question should not be easily answered—"yes" or "no." It should request specific expression, since that is our goal—to get him to reply in such a way that he expresses the idea we want him to have.

The question may be quite general or it may be quite specific, as we will show in some of the examples which follow.

The Sales Situation

Salesmen use this technique with skill. Early in the interview an experienced salesman will ask questions such as: "What is your biggest problem with. . ." and then he refers to an area that is related to his product. It may be inventory, it may be delivery, it may be service. He never gets an answer that will not be helpful and often he gets an answer that expresses a need for a sales appeal that he wants to point up.

A more general type of question might be used by a customer-oriented automobile salesman. While he would prefer not to ask such a question as: "What problems have you had with the car you're driving?", he may readily take the opposite tack and ask: "What do you like most about your (name of car)?" The typical prospect may not dwell very long on what he likes about the car and often may swiftly move to a discussion of some of the things he doesn't like. When the salesman shows that these problems have been corrected in the new cars, the prospect feels that getting a new car is his own idea.

The Supervisory Situation

This technique is used by supervisors who want to get a maximum of motivation from subordinates by having them feel a sense of participation in decision-making. I know one foreman, with an excellent record in industrial relations, who always gets "the boys" together when a change has to be made in his department. After stating the problem, he asks: "How do you think this can be handled?" The important point is that he knows, already, the best way to handle it. He also knows that to get the most out of his subordinates, he must have them feel that they have a part in making the decision.

In the case of a dispute or grievance, a foreman may ask: "What does the union contract say about that?" This forces the disputant to state it (or look it up) and accept the idea as his own.

The Personal and Home Situation

Suppose you'd like to stay home and watch television, but you think some of your "crowd" might want to go to a dance. Question: "What's on TV tonight?"

Your son wants the car to go out on a school night. You know that he hasn't been doing well in chemistry. You also know that chemistry classes are every day of the week. A good question? "What classes do you have tomorrow?" When he mentions chemistry, the next question comes: "Have you got your chemistry lesson?"

When the invitation to the "big" party comes, why not ask your wife: "What happened to that pretty blue satin dress you got last fall?"

Get The Right "Mental Set" For Questioning

Make the questioning approach to the presentation of your ideas a mental habit and you soon will develop skill in getting others to express your ideas for you!

E-3   Discuss A General Situation Touching On (Or Relating To) The Idea Until The Other Person Expresses The Idea

Many times, discussing things that are general but related to an idea that we want to put over will cause the other person to express the idea we want to put across. It may not come out in the exact words we would have used. It may not be the exact idea that we want to put across. A little re-wording and more emphatic statement of the idea will give it the flavor you want, but the other person will still feel that it's his idea.

The Sales Situation

A salesman enters the Purchasing Agent's office and says: "It sure looks as if you people are awfully busy around here." The Purchasing Agent may then talk about problems of delivery and supply, giving the salesman his opening.

In using this technique, you should be patient. Let the other person talk. Don't worry about it—he will! You wait him out, listening carefully. The Purchasing Agent (above) may take quite awhile to reach the idea that the salesman wants him to express. There may be some interchange and the salesman may have to go back to E-2 and ask an appropriate question.

The Supervisory Situation

After an industrial accident, a supervisor may talk about it at a coffee break and get the group discussing it. Someone in the group will show that a violation of safety rules was (or may have been) involved. The supervisor uses this as a platform or springboard for a re-affirmation of the importance of industrial safety.

A supervisor who is trying to get his subordinates to become more cost-conscious can start a conversation about inflation in a general way. There is likelihood that some employee may then make reference to rising costs facing the company.

The Personal or Home Situation

The same technique applies in personal, social, or family situations. Talking about a general subject may cause the person you want to influence to express your idea or something close to it.

Suppose you are trying to get your child to spend less time watching television. "You know," you say in front of the family group, "Dr. Jones (the eye doctor) says that watching a movie—or television, which is the same thing, is one of the most tiring visual tasks. Tires out your eyes more than almost anything." In the ensuing conversation the question of how much television watching can be done without tiring the eyes may be expressed by your child.

Suppose the "crowd" wants to go to a dance, but you'd rather they'd stay at the house and watch television. You mention that there was a funny incident on a show that took place just a week ago (without saying so). "I thought I'd die when they pulled that gag about Elizabeth Taylor on the 'Laugh-Off' show. . ." Someone is likely to inquire about what night that show comes on and—there it is, right in *TV Guide*— tonight!

To Get The Most Out Of This Chapter

To set these techniques in your mind, write down the letters "A", "R", and "E" on separate lines of a piece of note paper.

After "A" write—"*Assume* he accepts the idea."

After "R" write—"*Relate* the idea to his previous behavior or previously expressed ideas."

After "E" write—"Get him to *express* it himself."

Now go back through A-1, A-2, and A-3, and write out an example of each of these three techniques:

A-1—Offer a choice, either of which means he accepts the idea.

A-2—Assume acceptance of the idea by using a word such as "When. . .," "After. . .," or "As. . ."

A-3—Remind the other person of the idea as if he already knew it.

Then start out on the R's:

R-1—Relate the idea to his previous behavior or previous expressions.

R-2—Relate the idea to something he said (as if this had suggested it).

Then finish off with the E's:

E-1—Make notes to show how a series of facts will lead to a conclusion you want the other person to express.

E-2—Think of several questions, the answer to which will stimulate the expression of an idea.

E-3—Think of general areas of discussion which may prompt a person to express your idea or something close to it.

Important

To develop the maximum of expertise in these techniques, get into the habit of using them in all of your life situations. If you are a salesman, don't forget to use them in your family and social life. If you're a supervisor, the same is true. If you use these techniques in *all* life situations, you will make them a part of you!

Chapter Five

HOW TO USE
THE NEED FOR PERSONAL WORTH
IN PRESENTING YOUR IDEAS

The need for a feeling of personal worth is one of the most powerful and ever-present sources of motivation. It is dependable. It is always there within the consciousness of that other person, awaiting and demanding satisfaction.

We could use the word "importance" as a synonym for personal worth, but it would fall short of the full implication that we find in the two words "personal worth." Importance implies bigness in the minds of others, while personal worth may be wholly intrinsic. A thing which enhances an individual's personal worth may not make him seem more important to others.

In the face-to-face situations in which you present an idea to another person, his personal worth looms large. Accepting your idea without qualification or addition on his part makes him seem "little," makes you seem "big."

We showed in Chapter Four that one of the most effective ways to get acceptance for your idea is to make the other person feel it was his idea all the time. This is usually the surest way—the ARE techniques, which involve (1) Assuming that he has accepted the idea, (2) Relating the idea to his previous behavior and background, and (3) Getting him to express the idea.

ARE Techniques Are Not Always Available

While they are best, the Assuming, Relating, and Expressing techniques cannot be used in all situations. There are times when none of the three types will work, not because they have weaknesses, but because the time and subject matter do not permit it.

While this is especially true in "cold" situations where you have little or no information about the other person, it can be true in any face-to-face situation in which the other person has rejected your (A) Assumption of acceptance, has not given information that (R) Relates to the idea, or has proved unresponsive to your effort to get him to (E) Express the idea.

Under these circumstances the idea must be presented in such a way that it is not *his* idea, but yours.

Also, these additional techniques provide "change of pace."

Build Up Or Protect His Personal Worth!

In such cases we have techniques which are designed to (1) build up his sense of personal worth before presenting the idea, or (2) protect his feeling of personal worth before presenting the idea.

We have five techniques which fall into this category. Three of them use the Build-Up method, so we will label them "B." Two more protect his sense of personal worth by making it seem that the idea came from some Other source than you. We'll call them "O" techniques. Later, in Chapter Six, we'll add two more types of techniques with the letters "L" and "D" to identify them. To help you remember, these spell the word "BOLD" to indicate that these are the "Bolder" ways to present ideas as opposed to the ones that we learned in Chapter Four.

Here Are The Three "B" Techniques

Let's list the three ways that we use the Build-Up for presenting our ideas:

B-1 We reduce (diminish) our own personal worth to make him feel bigger, more important.

B-2 We pay him a sincere compliment before presenting the idea.

B-3 We ask permission to present the idea.

Here Are The Two "0" Techniques

Then there are the two additional techniques which make it seem as if the idea came from some Other source:

0-1 We present the idea as if it came from some Other person.

0-2 We present the idea as if we were talking to some Other person (or to people in general).

THE "BUILD-UP" "B" TECHNIQUES

B-1 We Reduce (Diminish) Our Own Personal Worth To Make Him Feel Bigger, Then Present The Idea

In every face-to-face situation each person wants to feel that his own personal worth is at least as great as that of the person he faces. Each of them is subconsciously striving to build up his own personal worth in any interchange.

For this reason, any expression of humility, modesty, or self-abasement makes the other person feel a greater sense of personal worth. He becomes more receptive, more willing to accept the idea that has been expressed following such an introduction.

You may be able to fix this more clearly in mind by thinking of the face-to-face situations as a "Teeter-Totter." When two youngsters face each other on a teeter-totter, one goes up when the other goes down. Similarly, if you lower your own personal worth through expressions of humility, you raise the other person!

It is sometimes difficult for younger, well-educated individuals to see the wisdom of this technique. They feel that self-abasement or modesty diminishes their personal worth to the point where it interferes with effectiveness. They may feel that it reduces the respect of their subordinates.

The important thing for them to realize is that the modesty, humility, or self-abasement is not *general* or *total*. The words used apply to the specific situation in which the other person actually has some greater knowledge, experience, or aptitude.

Examples should make this clearer.

The Sales Situation

Many salesmen must work with prospects who have more technical knowledge or more experience than they. Machine tool salesmen must work closely with engineers, yet most of them are not engineers themselves. I have talked to several of them who use this as an effective build-up. . . ."You're the engineer. You probably understand better than I why this particular feature of our milling machine has caused it to be so popular with companies like yours."

A car salesman could say to a traveling salesman: "You know a lot more about turnpike driving than I do—you probably drive three turnpike miles to my one. As a result you can see why we have developed this new steering assembly."

The high-fashion sales girl could say: "Of course I don't go to any of the big parties at the club like you do, but it seems to me that this dress would be ideal for that type of wear."

The Supervisory Situation

A supervisor might say: "When I started to work here the stamping machines were not nearly as complicated as the one you work with. The machine I used was pretty simple, compared to the ones we have now. As a result, I think you can see why the best way to handle this particular stamping is . . ."

In working with modern college-trained management recruits, older men can reduce the worth of their college training to heighten the personal worth of the younger men. "When I was in school they didn't . . . " "When I studied investments there was no SEC to complicate the market . . . " The successful executive who did not go to college or complete his education can always use this as a source of humility in working with college men. "I didn't go to college . . ."

It's well to keep in mind that this ties in with the "multiplier" idea if the other person *has* what you *don't* have. When you say "I'm not an engineer" to an engineer—that's a "multiplier" of a minor type. The same is true of "I'm no statistician" in talking to a person who prides himself on his statistical knowledge and "I'm not an accountant" to the accountant.

The Home and Personal Situation

A man might say to his wife: "I don't have much taste when it comes to judging women's clothes at parties, but I sure could see how your blue satin party dress drew a lot of compliments."

A mother might say to her child: "When I went to school there wasn't nearly as much to learn as there is today, so it didn't take as much time for homework. Now there's so much more to learn that it makes homework that much more important. You should finish your homework before you start watching television."

A father might say to his son in high school: "We didn't have two cars in the family when I went to high school. As a result, I didn't get to use the family car very often. It didn't interfere with our homework in those days, either. I think using the car on week nights should depend on how well you're doing in terms of grades. Take chemistry, for example. . ."

Remember: When you reduce your own personal worth, you build up the other person's. It's like the teeter-totter—when you go down, he goes up!

B-2 We Pay The Other Person A Sincere Compliment, Then Present The Idea

A person is more receptive if some phrase or sentence builds up his personal worth before we ask him to accept an idea. The big factor in this technique, however, is the word "sincere". Flattery is negative because it implies that the person is so vain that he will accept it. As a result, flattery should never be used (except in a humorous vein).

The sincere compliment that shows that we have knowledge of accomplishments, prestige or possessions of the other person will make a very good preface to the presentation of an idea. This is especially true where a "multiplier" may be involved—something in his background which makes him want to accept the idea.

We can show the difference between flattery and a sincere compliment by going back to the example of Roy Wood and the refrigerator sale in Chapter Three. Had he simply said to the wealthy prospect: "You're smart—you're successful in business and you know the value of a product made by a leader in the field. . ."—that would have been flattery.

But Roy Wood had already listened to the wealthy prospect's analysis of a bet against the Yankees. He knew that the man calculated odds and made his purchases shrewdly. As a result, his reference to the earlier discussion about the bet was a sincere compliment and not flattery.

The Sales Situation

A car salesman might say to an accountant: "You're the type of person who deals with figures and expects them to be exact, so you will be interested in the actual field-testing studies showing what it costs to operate our compact models."

On the other hand, a car salesman might present the idea of a deluxe model to a medical doctor with words like these: "As a hard-working doctor, you need a car that relaxes you and gives you dependable transportation. Also, as a respected professional person you want to avoid ostentation. This top model in our line gives you all the comfort and capacity of a Cadillac, but it isn't thought of as a 'rich man's car.' "

A sales lady in a dress department might say: "From the dress you're wearing, I can see that you like tailored things and I must say your taste is good. Let me show you one of our new fall dresses which fits right in with your taste for tailored designs."

Salesman talking to a purchasing agent: "You and your firm are known throughout the country as careful judges of O.E.M. (Original Equipment Manufacturer) materials, so I think you'll see how our line of controls will not only meet your quality standards, but fit right into your production sequences."

The Home and Personal Situation

Again we might take the case of the Johnsons' party and the new dress problem, with the husband saying: "You were the best dressed gal at that party last winter when you wore that blue satin to the Williams' open house. Why not wear it to the Johnsons'?"

The sorority president might say to an alumna: "You have such an attractive home and patio that the girls were hoping we might have our rush party there. . ."

To suggest to another couple that they might help to get a new young executive and his wife better acquainted in their new home town: "You and your wife know so many of the nice younger couples around town that George and I wanted you to meet his new assistant and his wife . . . "

It is important to remember that "sincerity" is the key word. The compliment must be real and it must build up personal worth.

B-3   We Ask Permission To Present The Idea

If a person has given us permission to present an idea, he is more receptive than if the idea is presented without such permission. The mere fact of asking permission protects his personal worth in all cases, but also builds it up when the technique is used skillfully.

As we noted earlier, this can become a technique which is used too often or too much. Some people develop a trite (for them) phrase and seem to "harp" on it. "May I say something?" or "May I make a suggestion?" can begin to sound like a broken record if it is always used in the same way and with the same inflection. The technique should be used sparingly and with different ways of asking permission. The examples give several different ways to ask permission. Some of them do not actually ask permission in so many words, but imply the request just the same.

The Sales Situation

An appliance salesman, with a refrigerator prospect, might say: "Would you be willing to let me show you how our compressor works and why it is so economical? We have a cut-away model right over here."

A car salesman could say: "If you would be willing to look for a moment at this drawing of our X-omatic transmission, it would give you an understanding of the difference between it and that type you are driving. Now, the reason it is more economical in terms of gasoline mileage comes from. . ."

A machine tool salesman might ask permission in a subtle way by saying: "You're very busy and I don't want to take too much of your time, but this set of figures shows how our new shaper has effected economies for two other companies and it won't take five minutes to go over it. O.K.?"

Some salesmen have a feeling of resistance when it comes to "order blanks." I know of a car salesman who gets permission from his prospect before filling out a "tentative" order blank. "If you would permit me to get one of our order blanks and fill it out tentatively, it will be easier to see how the features we have talked about will affect the total trade difference. . ."

The Supervisory Situation

A supervisor might say: "Have you got a minute? I'd like to take you back to my office and show you. . ."

Executive to management trainee: "Would you like to see what Peter Drucker says about how the effective executive conserves his time?" He then reaches for the book and begins to quote. It is worth noting that he is combining B-3 with 0-1 (following).

There are many phrases which express this technique in supervisory situations: "May I show you an easier way to do that?" "Would you be interested in seeing. . .?" "There's a short-cut that can be used in figuring that problem. Would you like to see it?"

The Home and Personal Situation

A father might say to a child whose grades are a little low: "Would you let Dad show you why it's important to make good grades?"

In soliciting a church pledge, one might say: "Would you let me show you how the church budget will stack up for next year?"

A college counsellor, talking to a student who is making grades below his predicted level, might say: "Have you ever seen the research studies showing the relationship between hours of study time and college grades?"

"No, I've never seen them."

"Would you mind letting me show you how it works?"

Summarized, it never hurts to ask permission to present an idea. This technique may be used in combination with others, too. It can follow a B-1 or B-2 approach.

THE "O" TECHNIQUES—THE IDEA COMES FROM
SOME "OTHER" SOURCE

These techniques simply protect the other person's feeling of personal worth in the face-to-face situation by preventing any inference that it is *my* idea and not *yours.* When the idea is presented with a preface using one of these two techniques, there is no loss of personal worth to the other person.

0-1　We Present The Idea As If It Came
From Some Other Person

We can often present an idea as if it came (or actually came) from some other person.

In B-3, above, we combined this technique with the primary B-3 technique of asking permission in the case in which the quote from the Peter Drucker book was used. Permission was obtained first, then the idea was presented as the author's idea, not the "boss's" idea.

There are some necessary words of caution about its use, however. First, if you name a specific person (testimonial, perhaps) you must be sure that the person is respected or, at least, not disliked, by the person to whom the idea is presented. If the other person will not accept the idea of the named person, you are worse off than if you had not used this technique at all!

Second, this technique should not be used as a "buck passing" device. In work or supervisory situations if you say, "The boss says. . ." it may sound as if you are simply relaying the boss's ideas and not necessarily accepting the idea as good. In social or home situations it is not wise to use the name of some other person whose authority to speak on that point may be questioned. If we quote a movie star on some social or family problem, we may get the response, "What does he know about that?"

The Sales Situation

A car salesman says: "One of my customers who bought this model has already sent three other people to me. He likes it that much!"

Or: "A customer was asking me the other day what the difference is between our X-omatic shift and other automatic transmissions. So I showed him this drawing."

A machine tool salesman has many opportunities to put over an idea by showing how his machine has helped other customers. However, such salesmen should avoid citing the use of the machine by a direct competitor. "While your business is making air conditioners, let me show you how one of our appliance manufacturers is using this type of control."

There are many simple little phrases which can be brought into use in this technique—"As one of my customers was saying. . .," "When one of my customers asked me. . .," "One of the people who came to our booth at the Home Show said. . ."

The Supervisory Situation

Supervisor to workman (to put across the idea of company benefits): "One of the new employees was asking me about his benefits here and how they compared with the ones he had at the Acme Company. Here's what I showed him. . ."

Again, there are many phrases which can be brought to bear on this technique—"One of the other operators was faced with the same kind of situation and he worked it out this way. . ." "One of the other fellows did it like this. . ." "A supervisor in the 410 department found out that the best way to handle this is. . ."

The Home or Personal Situation

A parent might say to a child in school: "One of the mothers at the PTA meeting the other night told us how her daughter did her homework first, then watched TV."

Or a teacher might say to a parent: "Several of the mothers mentioned at the last PTA meeting that 'they used a TV program as a reward for getting the homework out of the way first."

Suppose you want to get the crowd to go to a certain show? "Some of the fellows at the office were saying what a good time they had when they went to the current show at the Cinee Theater." Quoting a review of a show or a television repeat might prevail on someone to watch it with you.

You can use phrases such as: "One of the fellows says. . .," "Like Charlie was saying. . .," "As (name of a columnist) says, you can't always count on. . ."

0-2 We Present The Idea As If We Were Talking To Some Other Person OR To People In General

In some cases it is not even necessary to attribute the idea to someone else in order to protect the other person's feeling of personal worth and induce more receptivity. We can appear to be talking to someone else or we can seem to be "just talking." While an idea presented in this way carries some feeling of the vague or indefinite mood, it is easy and useful at times.

The Sales Situation

A car salesman might introduce the idea of the particular transmission in his auto line by saying: "Sometimes I wonder if motorists really understand how the different automatic transmissions work. Now this drawing. . ."

Another variation of the same idea: "A person who realizes how complex an automatic transmission is, can understand why they cost more. Now this drawing shows. . ."

A sales person in a dress department might say: "When a person who is quite slender asks me what type of lines would do the most for her figure, I explain it this way. . ."

Salesman to purchasing agent: "I often think about how much money is wasted because manufacturers of sub-assemblies don't field-test their products right in the customer's plant."

The Supervisory Situation

A supervisor might say to a union man who is talking about filing a grievance: "If a new employee asks me why the contract limits the filing of grievances to two weeks after the occasion, I show him what would happen if there were no limitations. The situation would become real bad."

Office manager to new stenographer: "If a person makes an erasure on an inter-office memo, it makes no difference. But if it is on a sales letter, we do it over because . . ."

Executive to management trainee: "When a person stops to think about it, management of time is one of the most important things to learn around a business."

The Home and Personal Situation

Father to son: "When you pick up the paper and see how many accidents happen to teen-agers, you realize the importance of careful driving. . ."

A mother to daughter: "Sometimes a girl doesn't think arithmetic is important, but when you have your own bank account . . ."

Fraternity rush captain to freshman: "When our fraternity looks at the new freshmen coming to school, we're especially interested in men who have been class officers—like you."

You'll see many phrases in the above examples that can be used frequently, such as:

"Sometimes I wonder. . ."
"I often think. . ."
"If a person stops to think. . ."
"Sometimes a person. . ."

Any such phrases tend to "soften" the presentation of any idea to another person and protect his feeling of Personal Worth.

To Get The Most Out Of This Chapter

In this chapter we have studied techniques which are designed to build-up (B) the other person's feeling of personal worth before presenting the idea or to make it seem that the idea came from or was directed to some other (0) person.

Think of "B" for Build-Up and "O" for Other. In the next chapter we will describe some techniques which use the letters "L" and "D" as code letters. The four types of techniques in these two chapters will spell the word BOLD. It will help us to remember that these are the techniques which are more *bold* than the ARE techniques which *are* usually the most effective.

On a piece of paper, write the letter "B" for "build-up." Then farther down the page write the letter "0" for "other" people.

Under the "B" write:

B-1
B-2
B-3

Then try to remember what B-1, B-2, and B-3 techniques were and write this down after the code words. Check with the text of this chapter to see how well you remembered. Then correct your interpretation, if necessary.

Now write an example of each of the "B" techniques for each of three situations: Sales, Business, and Social (or Home). This means you will end up with nine examples of the B techniques. In three of them you will build up the other person's sense of personal worth by diminishing your own worth. In three more you will use a sincere compliment as the build-up. In these you should be sure to think of real people and compliments that you know are genuine and deserved. Your last three "B" examples will achieve the build-up by asking permission to present the idea.

Now take another piece of paper and write the letter "O" with the word "Other" after it.

Try to remember what the two "O" techniques are and then check your text to see if you have remembered them correctly.

Now write out examples of each of the two "O" techniques, one for Sales situations, Business, and Home or Personal.

You should end up with six "O" examples. There will be three in which you present the idea by having it seem to come from some "other" person. Another three will make it seem that you are presenting the idea to some other person or to people in general.

See how many phrases you can think of that are suited to O-2. Phrases will be words such as, "If a person stops to think. . ." and "Sometimes I wonder. . .", etc.

Remember To Practice Them In All Situations

Don't forget that you want to use these techniques in *all* situations. Practice them on your children, your spouse, your fellow workers, your bridge club, your bowling team, your Sunday School class. . . .make everybody you meet a "guinea pig" for you to practice on!

Chapter Six

HOW TO USE

THE LOSS OF PERSONAL WORTH

AS A FORCE IN PRESENTING YOUR IDEAS

In Chapter 5 we showed five ways to get acceptance of ideas by building up personal worth or at least protecting the personal worth of the other person.

These were "B" techniques (which build up personal worth) and "O" techniques (which protect personal worth by making it seem that the idea comes from others or is directed toward others).

We said that we were going to add "L" techniques and "D" techniques to spell the memory-aid "BOLD"–the BOLDer techniques.

The "L" techniques are those which make the other person feel that he will lose personal worth if he does not accept an idea we present.

The "D" techniques are ones which use disagreement as the means to force acceptance. If a person is stimulated to express disagreement in such a way that it requires acceptance of an idea, we have achieved our goal.

So it's L for loss of personal worth by not accepting and it's

D for disagreement. In slightly different ways they both involve Loss of personal worth if the idea is not accepted. We can think of them also as *forcing* techniques. We are now forcing the person to protect his feeling of personal worth by accepting the the idea.

Forcing Is Dangerous

These "L" and "D" techniques are dangerous, intrinsically. No one likes to feel threatened or forced in a face-to-face situation.

In some situations, the person who is threatened with a loss of personal worth by refusing to accept, may "shift field" on you and claim that his personal worth will not be affected, that it will not apply in his case. Also when we try to force disagreement, we may wind up by having the person agree with us under some circumstances. This spoils the technique.

As a result, these techniques must be very skillfully and very cautiously used. Also, they must be used sparingly. The important thing, in each technique, is to know the person so well that you have powerful odds in your favor. This is more specially true of the disagreement techniques. You must be *sure* that he will disagree with you. To be sure, you must have studied the other person very carefully and be positive about his tendency to disagree.

Never Use These Techniques In Such A Way
That Argument Is Started

There is another intrinsic danger in the "L" and the "D" techniques. They may start arguments. As we will show in Chapters Eight, Nine, and Ten, the cause is lost if an argument is started, unless the end result permits the other person to win the argument. One of the "D" techniques may sometimes start an argument which the other person appears to win. This, of course, is a way to get the idea accepted.

Here Are The Four "L" Techniques

There are four ways to present an idea in such a way that the other person will lose personal worth if he does not accept:

L-1 We show the failure or loss suffered by a person who did not accept the idea.

L-2 We compliment the other person but show that he will not merit the compliment in the future if he does not accept the idea.

L-3 We describe the type of person he would like to be but show that he cannot be that person unless he accepts the idea.

L-4 We show the consequences of failure to accept the idea so as to force acceptance.

Here Are The Two "D" Techniques

There are two ways in which "D" (for disagreement) techniques may force acceptance.

D-1 We express the opposite of the idea in such a ridiculous way that he will disagree.

D-2 We express the opposite of the idea in such a way as to start an argument which he "wins" by accepting the idea.

THE "L" TECHNIQUES—HE LOSES PERSONAL WORTH IF HE DOES NOT ACCEPT

L-1 We Show The Failure Or Loss Suffered By A Person Who Did Not Accept The Idea

If we cite how a person failed or suffered a loss because he did not accept an idea, the other person senses that he will lose personal worth if he does not accept it. It is important that there be a clear-cut relationship between the situation we cite and the situation in which the techniques are used.

An example of how this technique could be used with negative results would be one in which a salesman tried to "hurry" his prospect by stating that this particular model is the last one in stock (the prospect will lose his chance to buy it unless he accepts the idea of buying now). The prospect, if not definitely committed to that model might say: "Well, I'm in no hurry, anyway. I intend to look around." Result: The prospect gets away and probably buys somewhere else.

This is a negative example and does not imply that the technique might not work in other cases. This salesman's mistake lay in not being sure that the customer was in a hurry for a new car and primarily interested in that model. Had he been in that state of mind the technique might have worked.

We will try, through examples, to show situations in which this technique would be valuable.

The Sales Situation

A high-fashion sales lady might say: "I can see that you like this dress and it does look good on you. However, it's an exclusive and I had another good customer who put off taking an exclusive model. When she came back it has been sold."

An automobile salesman who has a prospect who is interested in air conditioning and who asks about installing it later might say: "Oh yes, you can add air conditioning later, but I had a customer last year who decided to wait and when hot weather came he had to wait several weeks until we got it in stock and could install it. Everybody gets behind on air conditioning in the hot months."

An automobile salesman might also use this technique to sell the larger engine: "One of my customers who decided against the big engine was very disappointed when he took a vacation in the mountains. . ."

In talking to a purchasing agent, a salesman might offset price competition by saying: "We lost a customer last year because of pricing, but he was back with us in six months because he needed our prompt service and delivery."

The Supervisory Situation

A Safety Engineer, trying to put across the idea of wearing safety glasses, might say: "We had this fellow who would not wear his safety glasses and he lost an eye as a result."

A supervisor might say to a management trainee: "One of our college recruits couldn't see the value of managing his time. The wage and salary committee left him without a raise for over two years."

Or a Sales Manager could put across the idea of prompt call reports by saying: "You know, one of our men lost a trip to Bermuda because he was always late with his reports. In a contest, you know, we have to live strictly by the rules. If he had built the habit of getting his reports in promptly he wouldn't have lost out."

The Personal or Family Situation

A parent, trying to drive home the importance of careful driving might say: "Remember how Jack lost his license when he got his third speeding ticket. Now, you've got two in two months and you'll have to drive without any infractions for 10 months."

A husband, trying to avoid the cost of a new dress might say: "All the fellows laugh at Helen Jones because she never wears a party dress twice. Call her a 'clothes horse.' "

A teacher, trying to emphasize the importance of outside reading: "Two years ago we had a student who could have made an 'A' if he had done his outside reading. He couldn't see it and we had to give him a 'C'. This pulled his average down and he couldn't get into the college he wanted."

L-2   We Compliment The Other Person But Show That He Will Not Merit The Compliment In Future If He Does Not Accept The Idea

As in the case of B-2 (previous chapter) the compliment must be sincere and there must be a real likelihood of loss of personal worth if the idea is not accepted.

The Sales Situation

Automobile Salesman: "You mentioned that you had a perfect accident record. That's not only something to be proud of, but it saves you on your insurance rates. However, with everybody buying power brakes and an increase in the popularity of disc brakes you may not be able to keep that perfect record without disc brakes. In tight traffic situations you have to be able to stop as fast as the car in front of you."

Another automobile salesman might say: "You told me that you got a lot of brownie points from your wife when you put power brakes on your present car. The first time she learns about power steering she's going to wonder why you didn't add that option to this car. It's especially popular with the ladies— they don't have the strength to turn the wheel in parking."

A salesman who is trying to meet price competition could say: "Your company has an excellent reputation for quality control and it has helped your growth. Admittedly, our machine is higher than the competition by a small amount, but if it helps you maintain your reputation for quality control it will more than pay for itself."

The Supervisory Situation

Most supervisors get a chance to learn about the things that cause subordinates to feel a sense of personal worth. They can use this knowledge to make this technique work.

Supervisor to workman: "When you were actually operating a machine you were always a very careful workman. Now that you're going to be the set-up man for this department, you want to be sure that you keep that reputation."

Supervisor to a "trouble maker": "You and I have always been able to talk things out in a spirit of frankness. I hope we can continue that kind of relationship now that you're the shop steward. I'd appreciate it if you'd let me know first when there is some kind of grievance in the wind."

Executive to Management Trainees: "You made good grades in college, according to the records, and also had time for activities. You must have done a good job of budgeting your time in order to do that. The same thing applies in business—an effective management man needs to make the best and most efficient use of his time."

The Personal and Family Situation

Father to son: "Your principal told me last spring that your grades were good enough to make the Honor Society next year. But I've got news for you: It will be tough to do it if you get a 'D' in French."

Mother to daughter: "I've always said that my daughter was no problem to her parents. I won't be able to say that unless you're willing to accept the idea of being home by midnight on week ends and not have dates on school nights."

Father to son: "The boys on the basketball team say that they can count on you in a clutch. That's the real reason for setting a definite bedtime on week nights—You need rest to keep you in shape so you can help the team."

L-3   We Describe The Type Of Person He Would Like To Be, But Show That He Cannot Be That Person Unless He Accepts The Idea

While L-3 is quite similar in some respects to L-2, the principal difference lies in the fact that in L-2 the compliment refers to things that have happened in the past. L-3 refers to the personal worth involved in his hopes for the future. If you describe the type of person that you know the other individual would like to be and then indicate that he can't reach that goal unless he accepts the idea, he will see that he may lose personal worth if he does not accept the suggested idea.

It is not wise to name an actual person unless you are sure that he has respect and admiration for that person. Hence we usually describe a "type" of person, not a real person. However, if you are sure that the person is striving to equal some celebrity in his field there is no harm in naming the person.

The Sales Situation

A wholesale salesman might say to a franchised dealer: "You have always felt that the extra profits from.repeat business were worth working for—the customers who come back for their next purchase. The Factory recognizes that Service is one of the most important things in getting repeat business. That's why they gave us these check lists to fill out for each dealership. Now here are the things that showed up on your check list."

A high-fashion saleslady: "It's nice to feel, when you go to a big party such as the one you mentioned, that people will notice what you're wearing. Any woman feels that way. That's why I recommend the blue satin instead of the black crepe. Also the blue satin is an exclusive."

An automobile salesman: "You mentioned that our deluxe model sure looked good in your neighbor's driveway—that's why you came in to look at it. While I'm not suggesting that you copy him, I think you should know that he ordered the big engine. That little figure on the front fender shows that it's the 325-horsepower."

The Supervisory Situation

Field Manager to Management Trainee: "You told me that you'd like to get into the Home Office. Having been there, I can tell you that the fellows at Home Office dress very conservatively."

Batting Coach to Weak Hitter: "I've heard you say in the locker room that you wish you could hit like Cleon Jones of the Mets—.340 or better. Now, if you'll come out early for batting practice. . ."

The Personal and Family Situation

Husband to wife: "You said you'd like to have a family car with power brakes and power steering like the Jones'. I'm all for it, but we've got to cut down somewhere to do it."

Father to son: "You keep talking about wanting to go to Stanford University, and I hope you can make it. I understand that it takes a 'B' average to get any consideration at all out there. If you keep on making a 'D' in trig it will pull you down below a 'B' average."

Or: "You want to play football when you go to State. Now, college football players have to average 'C' to stay eligible and the time to start getting good study habits is now."

L-4   We Show The Consequences Of Failure To Accept The Idea So As To Force Acceptance

The consequences of failure to accept the idea may be shown by example, as in L-1 where we cited the failure of a person who did not accept the idea, or simply by describing the consequences of failure to accept it. This is the technique in L-4. It has its uses, especially under circumstances where no example can be cited, or where the example is hypothetical.

The Sales Situation

A refrigerator salesman could say: "Spring is the time to buy a refrigerator, especially if yours is old and out of warranty. You see, refrigerators are most likely to fail in the hot summer months. Then, in addition to costly repairs you lose a lot of frozen foods in the freezer compartment and other foods subject to spoilage like milk."

An automobile salesman who anticipates possible out-of-town competition could say: "We're the nearest dealer to your home and office. That makes it easier to get your new car serviced. While your warranty applies at any franchised dealership, you know that our mechanics are going to give the tops in service to a car that has the name of our dealership on it." (Note: the consequences are implied, not stated.)

The same high-fashion sales lady who mentioned the customer who had lost the chance to buy an "exclusive" model by putting it off, might have used the more direct method. "Remember that this is the only blue satin in that design. When it's gone—that's the last of it."

The Supervisory Situation

A Supervisor might say to a subordinate: "You know that we have to file a progress report (periodic review, appraisal) every six months on every employee. I don't want to have to put down on that report that you weren't wearing your safety glasses (hard hat, safety shoes) today."

An executive might say to a management trainee: "Meeting these deadlines is important on your job. While I might be able to overlook a missed deadline or two, my boss is going to know it if you miss a deadline on a project like this and that could affect your future."

A supervisor might say to a secretary or stenographer: "When there's an obvious erasure on a letter going to a customer it means the letter must be done over."

The Personal or Family Situation

In an effort to get the "crowd" to stay home from the drive-in and watch the TV movie, one might say: "If we go to the drive-in we won't be able to get drinks, while here at home we can have anything we want. I'll be glad to mix drinks during the commercials!"

A father might say to a son in college: "Remember, if you don't make your grades you can't get initiated into the fraternity."

Wife to husband (she wants that new dress!): "I don't want to look like a ragbag at the Johnsons' party because your boss and his wife are going to be there."

THE "D" TECHNIQUES WHICH EMPLOY DISAGREEMENT IN SUCH A WAY THAT ACCEPTANCE IS FORCED TO PRESERVE PERSONAL WORTH

As we indicated earlier we can use the two "D" techniques to force acceptance of an idea. D-1 carries the *opposite* of the idea to the ridiculous, forcing disagreement. D-2 uses some extreme statement to start an argument which the other person "wins" when we agree with him.

D-1   We Express The Opposite Of The Idea In Such A Ridiculous Way That The Other Person Will Disagree

If a person makes a statement of disagreement he must maintain his position or lose some personal worth. To get him to do this we may state the opposite of our idea in such a ridiculous way that it forces disagreement. We then agree with him. We all use this technique in social discussions or in "kidding," but it is dangerous unless very skillfully employed. Some persons, skilled in argumentation, may "trap" us by agreeing!

In logic this is called the "reductio ad absurdum"—reducing it to the absurd.

A salesman might make a mistake by saying: "I tell people who don't want a car with room and horsepower that they might as well buy a 'bug.' " And the prospect might reply: "You know that's a good idea. I hadn't thought of that."

I knew a professor who once said: "If you're not going to try to make a 'B' in this course you might as well drop it." And four of the students dropped the course!

Still, with caution and preparation, the D-1 technique will be useful at times.

The Sales Situation

A salesman might say to a purchasing agent: "Why bother to specify delivery dates on your purchase orders?" The purchasing agent then stresses the importance of delivery dates and their relation to factory production schedules. He makes them very important. Then the salesman comes back with proof that his company has never missed a delivery date. The implication is that other suppliers don't have as good a record. In any case he has convinced the other person that his company respects the importance of delivery dates as specified.

In opening a part of his presentation emphasizing the importance of horsepower in his automobile, a salesman might say: "Of course it may be that you never have to pass anyone on a two-lane highway." The customer disagrees and says that he has to do that frequently. "That's the time you need the extra horsepower—you don't need it for cruising—but that's the time it may save your life."

The high-fashion sales lady might say: "It probably doesn't bother you to go to a big party and find that someone else is wearing an exact copy of your dress." Most women will disagree, which gives opportunity to emphasize the fact that this is an exclusive model.

The Supervisory Situation

A supervisor who wants to get acceptance for the idea that safety shoes are important uses this method on a new employee. "In our department some of these heavy objects can drop and hit a man on the foot. If he doesn't wear safety shoes he might as well go barefoot. You want to go barefoot?"

In explaining the rules concerning promptness a personnel man who is providing orientation for new workers might say: "In some respects, a person who is going to be thirty minutes late might just as well not show up at all." The danger here is that he might leave the impression with some new workers that if something delayed them they should stay home!

In explaining benefits, a supervisor or personnel man might say: "Of course you might figure that the company ought to have no limits on sick leave." The other person might say that he couldn't see how the company could afford that. The supervisor then agrees and shows what the limits are.

The Personal and Family Situation

This technique is used by the radio announcements urging the use of safety belts in automobiles. "Some excuses for not wearing safety belts are good for broken arms. . .some are good for fractured skulls. . .etc."

A parent might say: "If you're not going to do your home work you might as well not go to school at all."

A mother might say: "If we don't have some definite time for you to get in at night, we might as well let you stay out all night." ·

I remember a poker game in which a player got irritated because one of the others was "bulling" the game, betting the limit and raising (he was somewhat intoxicated). The player said: "Would you like to take the limit off the game?" The drunk didn't want that and began to play more sensibly.

D-2   We Express The Opposite Of The Idea In Such A Way As To Start An "Argument" Which The Other Person "Wins"

This technique is useful with persons who always disagree (sometimes called negativistic personalities). It involves careful thought and preparation. Frequently there is a sequence of several exchanges before the other person "wins" the "argument". As in a chess game, we must keep in mind the next "move".

The Sales Situation

Here's an example which was used by a salesman of O.E.M. parts ("O.E.M." stands for "Original Equipment Manufacturers"—companies who make special equipment and sub-assemblies placed into products sold by the buying company). He knew that this purchasing agent was always prone to take a negative position with salesmen. He always knew more than the salesman, he was outspoken and even rude, could be counted on to oppose any statement made by a salesman.

Salesman: "Of course you don't have any problems with the installation of O.E.M. parts."

Purchasing Agent: "We don't? That's one of our big problems. We have to maintain a testing staff to check on the quality and our engineering staff has to work out special procedures to insure proper installation."

Salesman: "Yes, but that would be true of any O.E.M. product."

Purchasing Agent: "You're wrong again. Some of them are pretty uniform. Others come with wide variations in tolerances."

Salesman: "Suppose I told you that our record for our controls is less than one part in a thousand that has to be rejected by our customers."

Purchasing Agent: "Well, I just wouldn't believe it on your say-so. You'd have to prove that. I don't think you could."

This was what the salesman wanted—an invitation to present his figures. He went on: "I'm like you, I wouldn't believe it either. But here are the figures that came out of a field study made by our field service engineers. They're backed up by the signatures of engineers from our customer companies."

The Supervisory Situation

This supervisor knew that one of his men was creating dissatisfaction with one or two aspects of the company benefits. If the man had mentioned it to him, the technique would have been classified as opposition to a "wrong" idea (see later chapters). Instead, he had to use the technique to put across his point about the company benefits. He knew that the man was argumentative and negative.

Supervisor (at a coffee break): "You know, I think they ought to cut out all the benefits and pay the money out in wages."

Employee: "Sure—that's the way you think. You don't have a big family of kids. Yours are grown up. I need the hospitalization. But I'll tell you this: That $25.00 deductible on the hospitalization is bad. I just had to pay out $25.00 when my kid was sick. They ought to cut that out."

Supervisor: "Well, like I say: If they paid you the extra wages you could buy the kind of coverage you want—without the deductible."

Employee: "The hell I could! It takes the group rate to get it. Besides, I'd have to pay income taxes on the extra wages."

Supervisor: "I hadn't thought of that, but you're sure right. If you had to buy the hospitalization for yourself, counting the income tax costs and everything, the $25.00 deductible wouldn't amount to much. You'd still be saving a pile of money. Besides that, our benefits include. . ." He then made a recapitulation of all of the benefits provided by the company.

Years ago I worked with a man of the negative disposition. Unfortunately, he was on the staff of the company president and certain ideas had to clear through him before going to the president. Had I presented an idea in a typical way, he would have flatly opposed it. I had found that out! Then the idea would never get to the president (who was a receptive and perceptive person, eager to accept a good idea).

So I found that the way to get the idea through to the president was to say: "Here's a good idea but we could never get Martin F. (the president) to buy it." He would challenge me, offer to bet he could sell the idea. So I would make the bet and he would "sell" the idea to the president.

After one such incident I saw the president later at lunch and he smiled and said: "That's a pretty clever trick you played on Charlie." Then he handed me a dollar bill and said: "I'll pay the bet you lost."

The Personal Situation

Men who like to gamble on sports events use this technique to get better bets. They get a person with a known loyalty to a certain sports team to make bets that are worse than the regular betting odds by starting this kind of argument. Let me recount such an argument which I overheard. It was a week before the Kansas University-Missouri University football game.

Gambler: "Your Jayhawks (K.U.) are sure going to take a beating next Saturday."

Jayhawk Alumnus: "Oh, I don't know. You know the boys are always 'up' for the Missouri game. You may be surprised."

Gambler: "I'll bet you fifty dollars M.U. wins."

Jayhawk: "Well, that's silly. It's not an even bet. Every sports expert has picked M.U. to win."

Gambler: "O.K. I'll give you three points. How's that?"

Jayhawk: "You're called."

What the K.U. alumnus did not realize was that if he had gone to the nearest barber shop he could have gotten ten points! The argument warped his judgment and he felt that the concession of three points might be enough. Of course, he lost!

A mother used this skillfully with her daughter in getting agreement on the time she should be in after dates.

Mother: "I understand that most of your friends—the girls in your 'crowd'—have to be in by ten-thirty."

Daughter: "That's not true! I guess I should know—I'm with them on double dates. I don't know any of them that have to be in that early."

Mother: "Well, I understood that Susan Jones has to be in by 10:30."

Daughter: "Well, that may be true, but Susan doesn't get asked for hardly any dates. Besides, she's a square anyway. And when you go to a school dance that breaks up at 10:30, why, gee, the gang wants to go get a hamburger or a malt afterward. That's part of going to a dance!"

Mother: "O.K., but you ought to be able to get a hamburger or a malt in an hour and be home by 11:30—no later than 12:00."

Daughter: "I suppose so."

To Get The Most Out Of This Chapter

We have now finished our list of ways to present ideas to give them the maximum chance to be accepted by others. The order in which we have presented them ranges from the surest ways to the riskiest ways. However, even the "risky" ones presented in this chapter have their place and, under certain circumstances, may be the only techniques available.

You have had an explanation and some drill on the ARE techniques, which ARE the best because the other person feels the idea was his own. He feels it is his idea because you have Assumed (A) that he already had accepted it, or because it was Related (R) to a pattern of behavior that is his own, or because you were able to get him to Express (E) the idea.

Then we moved to the BOLD techniques, bolder because the idea is presented more directly, but only after a preliminary introduction which BUILT up (B) his feeling of personal worth, made it seem that that idea protected his sense of personal worth because it came from OTHERS (O), made it seem that he would LOSE (L) personal worth if he did not accept it, or produced a DISAGREEMENT (D) which forced acceptance.

Since you have already practiced all of the techniques except the L and D techniques in this chapter, we will work only with them at this point.

To set the "L" and "D" techniques in your mind, take a piece of paper and write "L" and after that write "He will LOSE personal worth if he does not accept".

Then force yourself to remember the four different "L" techniques by writing down

> L-1
> L-2
> L-3
> L-4

Refer back to your text if you cannot remember what each one is, but try first to put down what they mean. Next, take a separate piece of paper and put "L-1" at the top. Write out an example of three L-1 techniques, one each for the sales situation, the supervisory or business situation and the family or social situation.

Do this with L-2, L-3 and L-4.

Now do the same thing with the "D" techniques. However, when you begin to write your examples for both D-1 and D-2, think of a *person* that these techniques would fit. For example, in D-2 you must think of someone who is always or usually negativistic and who will challenge your statement.

Again, Practice!

Find situations in which you can practice these "L" and "D" techniques. Use them in everyday situations with people whose personalities are suited to this type of technique. This will eventually make your use of all of these techniques automatic. In addition, you'll learn to choose the right one!

Chapter Seven

HOW TO
DEVELOP POWER IN
OPPOSING NEGATIVE ATTITUDES

Each time we present an idea, we face the possibility that the other person may reject it by expressing an objection. Also, in face-to-face situations another person may express a negative attitude—a "wrong"* idea that he wants us to accept. If we are to develop power in dealing with people we must learn the techniques to use in opposing such ideas and such negative attitudes.

The more skill we develop in presenting ideas, of course, the less likely we are to face disagreement. The techniques we learned in previous chapters increase our power to get acceptance for our ideas. Nevertheless, full power cannot be achieved without the added skill needed to effectively oppose objections that may be presented. The same skill increases our power to overcome negative attitudes when they are expressed.

*In this book we use the word "wrong" to describe an idea that stands as an obstruction in your path as you deal with people. Such an idea may not be "wrong" ethically or morally. It may just be an objection or a delaying action. And remember: If it turns out to be "right" there will be times when *you* will accept it. You will change!

112

No One Wins "Arguments"

It has been said by many sales trainers: "Win an argument and lose a sale." While this is a clever expression of a fundamental truth in selling, the salesman who loses a sale has not won anything. He has *lost* something and won *nothing*.

No one wins an argument if his goal is to get acceptance.

Once an argument starts, both parties to the argument have their personal worth at stake. The longer the argument continues the less chance there is to get either party to "give in." Personal worth becomes so deeply involved that neither person can give in. When we remember that the need for a feeling of personal worth is the most powerful and ever-present source of motivation, we see clearly that "A man convinced against his will is of the same opinion still." Tear down personal worth by overpowering argument and you have lost a friend or made an enemy. Build up personal worth and you have made a friend.

Lawyers and debaters, you may say, actually win "arguments." Such arguments are more like prize fights. They are not designed to influence the participants—they are designed to impress the debate judges, the audience, or the jury! No lawyer or debater has ever been convinced by his opponent.

Power in opposing negative ideas, objectives or attitudes depends on skill in keeping the discussion below the level of argumentation.

The Difference Lies In "Techniques"

Just as we studied the ways to present ideas in such a way as to get acceptance, so we must learn the techniques for overcoming negative ideas or attitudes. We must "oppose" such ideas without appearing to oppose them. We must *convince.* We cannot convince by raising our voice, pounding the table, or simply presenting a welter of evidence without a skillful preface.

Like the techniques we have just studied for presenting ideas, the fundamental need lies in building up or protecting the other person's sense of personal worth. After we have done this we may present convincing evidence to *remove* the wrong idea or attitude.

Removing "Wrong" Ideas Is Like Surgery

Just as the surgeon must remove a threatening lesion or diseased organ, so we must remove the wrong idea. And just as the surgeon recognizes that pain is involved in removing offending tissue, so we must realize that there is pain involved in getting a person to give up an idea—even if it seems "wrong" to us.

The surgeon must administer some kind of pain killer before he starts cutting. A person writhing in pain could hardly go through a successful surgical operation.

The Techniques Are "Pain Killers"

The techniques we will study in this chapter and ensuing chapters are "pain killers." Sometimes they will seem as mild as an aspirin tablet, in other cases they may be as powerful as a total anaesthetic. Just as the surgeon skillfully suits the pain killer to the problem he faces, so you will develop skill in using the best and most readily available technique. Your choice of a technique may be based on the tenacity with which the other person holds on to the wrong idea or attitude. You may choose one which is particularly suited to the background of the other person.

Think Of The Techniques As A "Bridge"

It may be easier to employ an acronym to help remember the techniques we will learn.

These techniques actually constitute a "bridge" between the expression of the wrong idea or attitude and our effort to remove it from the other person's mind. Just as we learned not to present an idea bluntly in our previous studies, so we cannot oppose the other person flatly and openly. In between we have the "bridge" that protects personal worth, prevents arguments.

Let's see how the word "BRIDGE" can help us to remember these techniques.

BR I D GE

These combinations of the letters that spell "BRIDGE" can describe the techniques which we will use to oppose wrong ideas effectively.

The first two letters "BR" stand for Blame Removers. If we remove the blame for having the wrong idea, the other person is more likely to give it up. If we show that it was not his fault that he had a wrong idea, we have removed blame and made it easy for him to give up the idea without losing personal worth.

The next letter in "Bridge" is "I." This stands for "Inflaters" or for "Importance"—we bridge to our opposition of his idea or attitude by building up his personal worth. We "inflate" his sense of selfhood, feeling of importance. This is similar to the "B" techniques in presenting ideas.

Then we have the letter "D" which stands for Delay. If we can place a cushion of time or conversation between his expression of the wrong idea and our effort to change him, we have bridged the gap and prevented a loss of personal worth.

Finally, we have the letters GE which stand for "Get Embarrassing." In these techniques as in the "L" techniques of presenting ideas, we make it appear that holding on to the wrong idea will cause him to *lose* personal worth. We can also let the GE stand for "Go Easy," because these are the most dangerous techniques when not used skillfully. They should be a last resort, just as they are last on our list of four types of techniques. We can refer to these as "Forcing Techniques" because they force a person to give up his idea or lose personal worth.

Four Ways To Make The "BRIDGE"

So let's list these four ways, using their letter-symbols that spell "Bridge".

B
R . . . . Blame Removers
I . . . . Inflaters—They Build Up Importance
D . . . . Delaying Techniques
G
E . . . . Get Embarrassing, but Go Easy!

We will show you a total of 7 ways to remove blame. Then in later chapters we will provide you with 5 inflaters, 4 delayers and 4 ways to get embarrassing so that the other person will lose personal worth if he does not relinquish the idea.

THE BLAME REMOVERS

The seven ways in which we can remove blame as a bridge to opposing the idea are:

BR-1   Show that many people agree with his wrong idea.

BR-2   Blame yourself for the wrong idea.

BR-3   Show that it was natural and logical for him to have the wrong idea.

BR-4   Agree with the wrong idea, but show that others who are more informed will not.

BR-5   Show that you felt the same way until you learned better.

BR-6   Indicate that he has not had a chance to "think it through."

BR-7   Re-state the wrong idea nearer to your position.

These blame-removers are the very best techniques to bridge between the expression of the wrong idea and your opposition to it. If he feels no sense of blame for having a wrong idea or attitude, his personal worth is not at stake when he gives it up.

Moreover, these techniques are of a nature which often permits their use in combination with other bridging techniques. Sometimes we can use more than one blame-remover, too. The BR techniques are always helpful, even when others are used in the same bridging operation.

BR-1   Show That Many People Agree With The "Wrong" Idea

Many ideas which are negative (as far as we are concerned) may be widely-held misconceptions. When you encounter such a misconception, the mere fact that you show it is a misconception held by many people absolves the other person from blame for having expressed it. After you have made this bridge, you then proceed to present the correct idea.

The Sales Situation

A prospect for a new automboile has just said: "No, I don't want an automatic transmission. Costs you several miles per gallon in gasoline consumption."

The salesman removes the blame: "You know, I find that many of our customers feel that an automatic transmission wastes gasoline. I can understand why you feel that way. However, the amount of additional gasoline used is very small if the driver uses the transmission properly. The drivers who floorboard the accelerator every time a light turns green actually do waste gasoline, but those who get away to a normal start use very little more gas than with a standard transmission."

A Purchasing Agent has said to a salesman: "No, we can't buy from your company. You make the highest-priced controls in the industry." The salesman: "Most companies that I call on for the first time have that same idea. Our ads stress quality and we try to sell the top products in our line. But we have more than one line and we are very competitive in price for the company that's trying to shave costs in a very competitive market. Let me show you the lower end of our line of controls."

The Supervisory Situation

A supervisor has found a press operator who has tied back one of the safety controls on a press. He says: "Almost every operator who starts on this job feels that it is unnecessary to have dual controls and they want to tie one back as you have. They naturally feel that they can work faster and earn more bonus that way. The truth is: It is not only unsafe—might cause the loss of a finger, hand or arm—but with a little more training and effort, you can work just as fast with the dual controls."

Personnel Director to Employment Manager: "Yes, I realize that (this applicant for work) is a red-head. There are many people who feel as you do that red-headed people are hot-tempered. I asked an industrial psychologist if this was true and he showed me that scientific studies had proved that the color of a person's hair has no relation to his temperament."

The Family And Personal Situation

A daughter has objected to the "rules" her mother has laid down about her dating. She says: "Most girls your age feel that their parents don't allow them as much freedom as they should have. I read that in a book by a child psychologist. But Daddy and I have checked with some of the other parents and we are permitting you as much or more freedom in dating than most parents. I think you'll find we are more liberal than the average parents."

Here's one that I heard a prominent psychiatrist use when a person stated flatly that a person who suffered from a mental illness "would never be the same again." "That's a common misconception—that people never really recover from an attack of mental illness. The truth is that practically all of them recover thoroughly and are better people than they were before they became ill. They understand themselves and other people better as a part of the therapeutic process."

In general, it is safe to say that a person will be more willing to give up a wrong attitude or idea if we show that it is a common error to think as he does. The evidence that we use to dispel the wrong idea must be good (as we have shown in these examples), but the bridge to remove the blame is important to their acceptance of the "rebuttal."

BR-2   Blame Yourself For The Wrong Idea

This technique of removing blame is good because it reflects an attitude of humility and thus, also, elevates the other person's sense of personal worth. It is frequently useful when an objection has been raised to an idea previously advanced. If you accept the blame it is easy for the other person to give up the wrong idea.

The Sales Situation

The customer of an automobile salesman has said: "Yeah, but I've given up buying these new gadgets the first year they put 'em on automobiles."

The salesman replies: "When I mentioned that this new feature is new this year, I failed to explain that this feature, like all new additions, goes through our proving grounds and takes thousands of miles of abuse before it is added to the car. That assures that it will stand up when it gets out into service. This is our only protection against excessive warranty costs."

A salesman talking to a purchasing agent has met the objection that the price is too high. He replies: "Well, to tell you the truth, I got carried away talking to you about our new top line of products and forgot to mention that we have two other lines that are much cheaper. . .let me show you the way they are priced."

The Supervisory Situation

A workman has said that the Safety Rules are "a bunch of arbitrary ideas set up by some theoretical safety engineers." The foreman replies: "It's my fault that you feel that way because I just started talking about the rules as if they had been 'dreamed up' by our safety department. You see our plant industrial engineers keep extensive records about accidents and they study the cause of each one. Their long-range records, going back for years, establish the causes of accidents and they set the safety rules on the basis of that research. Now, take for example. . ."

A management trainee has objected to being transferred to a small branch in the field. His supervisor says: "We probably made a mistake and overlooked telling you that this is a part of our training. I presumed that the college recruiting staff explained this to you. I shouldn't have taken it for granted and should have told you myself. However, it is a part of our training program to give a little field experience to every college trainee. It will be for eighteen to twenty-four months, maximum, and then you'll come back into the home office."

The Personal And Family Situation

When a daughter has complained to her mother that the 12:30 curfew is arbitrary and embarrasses her when she is out with a "double date," her mother comes back: "Daddy and I didn't mean that we were going to expect you to open the front door at exactly 12:30. We knew that you couldn't tell the crowd that you had to be home in five minutes or ten minutes, even though we neglected to mention it. What we do expect is that you arrive home at about that time or call us and tell us why."

In trying to influence another's vote for a Congressional candidate, the other person objected, saying: "Well, you're a Republican and I just never vote for a party, I vote for a man."

In making the bridge, the Republican says: "Well, I'm registered as a Republican, but I sure didn't mean to ask you to vote for Jones because he's a Republican. I neglected to mention that as a Republican I am familiar with his record, and that's why I'm asking you to vote for him. For example. . ."

We can make an effective bridge to present our case for our point of view by taking the "blame" for the wrong idea.

BR-3 Show That It Was Natural and Logical For Him To Have The Wrong Idea

In some ways this bridge doubles over on BR-1 and BR-2 because common misconceptions (BR-1) and failure on our part to clarify (BR-2) may make it natural and logical for a person to have a wrong idea or attitude. However, BR-3 contains an added element: In BR-3, we tie our blame-removing technique to circumstances peculiar to the other individual and his way of life. Thus there are some elements of the "magic multiplier" in BR-3 because it links the blame removal to the other person's background in many cases.

The Sales Situation

A compact car salesman, talking to a man who is interested in a second car, finds that he is debating the possibility of buying a used car for the family "because a larger car has more comfort." "Since the company car that you drive is a long-wheel-base car with a lot of room, you have a natural tendency to feel that this compact will not be roomy enough or ride comfortably enough for your wife and daughter. However, you want to remember that your wife and daughter are not as big as you and that the shorter wheel base makes it easier for them to park a compact car. Let's let them try it out...it has good springing and should be comfortable."

Saleslady to a mother who wants to buy something cheaper because her children tend to outgrow their clothes: "I can see why you would feel that this (garment) is expensive because your child is at an age when he needs a new size every year or so. On the other hand, my experience with some of our regular customers would indicate that cheaper garments will wear out before they're outgrown and that makes them twice as expensive. Perhaps if we take a size that's slightly larger we'll stretch the useful life of this better garment..."

The Supervisory Situation

An executive has to correct a Management Trainee who has been too terse and brief in his instructions to subordinates. "As a man who graduated in the top ten per cent of his class you would have a natural tendency to think that people should understand instructions the first time they are expressed. They are clear to you, of course. But the people you are working with don't have your education and background. It takes follow-up and repetition to be sure they understand. If you don't follow-up and double-up on your instructions their mistakes are really your fault as much as theirs. They can't do it right if they don't understand..."

An employee has complained about a certain provision of the company benefits. "I have to pay as much family coverage as Charlie and he has five kids while we have none." The reply: "Sure, it's natural that that would seem unfair to you now while you have no children. But the rates are low because of the size of our group coverage and you couldn't duplicate them for the total cost. You only pay 50% of the total company outlay for coverage. Besides, don't forget that you'll get the benefits for your wife when she has a baby. And I don't think Charlie's going to have any more than five."

The Family and Personal Situation

The daughter who thinks she should be allowed to date on school nights, might get this BR-3 treatment from her mother: "It's natural for a girl like you who gets a lot of attention from the boys to feel that she should be able to accept every date, even on school nights. I can sure understand why you feel that way. The problem is, that you can't keep up with your homework when you're out to a movie. . ."

The mother of the groom has a very large list of wedding-reception guests, while the mother of the bride has a limited budget for the reception. "I can see why you and Arthur feel that you have to invite such a long list of guests to the reception. If I were in your position, I'd feel the same way. But Charles and I have stretched our budget to the maximum and we can't see how we can entertain more than 150 guests at the reception."

BR-4   Agree With The Wrong Idea, But Show That Others Who Are More Informed Will Not

It is not very often that we can agree with the "wrong" idea or attitude expressed by another, but when we can, it removes blame and provides the bridge to make your point in opposition. It has the advantage of putting you "on his side" and most certainly removes blame. Obviously the subsequent disagreement must be the opinion of those who know more, have more authority, are more expert.

The Sales Situation

An automobile salesman is faced with a customer who says that the same car, in a competing line, sells for a lower price. He replies: "Yes, their four-door sedan is priced lower than ours. I wish our price were as low or lower. It would make my work easier. However, we have sold our model to several very careful buyers including some fleet owners. Here's what they gave as their reason for preferring our car despite the higher price. . ."

The same technique can be used by any salesman who (a) does not have a certain model in his line; (b) does not have a feature that is shown in competing models; or (c) has a price disadvantage. Salesmen in this position lose no prestige by agreeing, but must be prepared to show other advantages that characterize their products or lines. It does remove blame and it does make the "bridge."

The Supervisory Situation

In manufacturing plants there are times when workmen disagree with a work standard as set by the industrial engineers or time study experts. Usually such disagreements are based on limited knowledge of the techniques used in setting such standards. The supervisor can agree with the worker, but then show the reasons behind the decision of the experts. "I feel much as you do. That standard seems high compared to the old one. But the engineers are able to show that the new machines we installed will make it possible to exceed that standard when we get used to them. . ."

A Chief Executive is opposed by his Sales Executive who objects to detailed reports required of his salesmen. "You know, I came up the sales route myself, and I agree with you that it's bad to take up a salesman's time filling out detailed reports. However, this year we need to do a lot of market research and this is the only way we can get some of the information we need. We'll simply have to sell the boys on the need for this data."

The Family And Personal Situation

A mother, who has a child just recovering from an illness and who wants to go to "the big game" might say: "I know you feel just as good as new and I can't see why we should make you stay home. But I talked to the doctor and he insists that with the kind of flu you had you must stay in for two days after you have had a temperature. He's the doctor, not me!"

This technique sometimes works in a humorous vein, too. For example, a partisan was in a political argument and his friend said, "But I think your candidate butchers the King's English."

He replied: "Yes, I admit he doesn't sound too good in his speeches, but as one of the men who knows him real well has said: 'We know he's honest and that's more than you can say about his opponent.' "

A story is told of a lawyer who used this technique effectively in defending a frontier newspaperman against a charge of libel and slander. His extreme dislike for the newspaper publisher made him refuse to say anything "good" about him, but his whole summary plea was based on agreement with the plaintiff's counsel that the newspaper man was vindictive and unwholesome. "But there is one man in this county who is worse—that man is the plaintiff!"

BR-5   Show That You Felt The Same Way Until You Learned You Were Wrong

Blame is always removed if we can show that we felt the same way until some clear or overwhelming evidence changed our opinion. This is especially true of commonly-accepted "wrong" ideas. While this technique is similar to BR-4, it is ideal for certain situations. It means that you have put yourself "on his side" of the argument in the past and that you only gave up the position he holds after learning better.

Actually, you are "dating back" your agreement to a prior time when you knew less about the subject.

The Sales Situation

An automobile salesman might meet the objection to an automatic transmission ("Uses too much gasoline") in this way: "You know, I felt the same as you do about that until I had a talk with our service manager. He explained why it is that some people waste gasoline with an automatic transmission. He asked me to change my driving habits for two tankfuls of gas. Sure enough, my mileage jumped two miles per gallon. He told me to accelerate normally from a dead stop and not floor-board the accelerator. So now, I take it easier when the light turns green and it saves a lot on gas!"

A high-fashion sales lady might face the objection: "But I have to pay that kind of price just to be sure that no one else has a dress like it."

She could remove the blame by saying: "I felt the same way until I had a chance to go to market. They showed me that the exclusive models are always made of better fabrics, have better sewing and trim. An exclusive model is actually a better dress in terms of quality and it will give that much better service at the same time that it continues to look dressy. . ."

Any salesman who has access to engineering information, field testing data, or other authoritative facts can use this technique. He felt the same way until he got facts.

The Supervisory Situation

In BR-4 we mentioned the supervisor who agreed that the work standard seemed high, but bowed to the opinion of the methods engineers. He might have used BR-5 and indicated that he felt the standard was unreasonable until he saw the data produced by the methods engineer. He might also say: "When I first came into this department I felt as you do. Then the company gave us some training in how the standards are figured and I could see that they are fair."

A Sales Executive went to a training seminar on accounting. Later when his Regional Sales Managers were complaining about "paper work," he agreed with them that he had felt the same way until he learned the significance of sales records in budgeting, forecasting, and market research.

Many executives use this technique in working with college-graduate management trainees. They admit that they felt the same way when they first graduated from college, but that experience has caused them to see things differently.

The Family And Personal Situation

Parents can use this technique skillfully by agreeing with their children that they felt the same way when they were at that age. A mother might say: "I thought my parents were too strict about rules and regulations when I was a teen-ager. Then when some of the girls whose parents weren't strict got into trouble, I realized that Mother and Dad were right. It wasn't because they didn't love me, it was because they really did love me and didn't want me to make a mistake."

When a person has received special training, he can remove blame by dating his agreement back to a time before he obtained that special knowledge. This works especially well when combatting common misconceptions. When a person tells me that red-headed people have bad tempers, I can always say: "I thought the same way until I went back to school to do graduate work in psychology."

BR-6   Indicate That He Has Not Had A Chance To "Think It Through"

Objections, wrong ideas, or attitudes that are expressed on the spur of the moment may be overcome by a "bridge" that removes blame by the suggestion that the individual has not had a chance to "think it through" to a more logical conclusion.

In some ways this is similar to the "D" techniques which involve delay, but the examples we are using here are primarily designed to remove blame and pave the way for getting conviction by "thinking it through" with the other person.

The Sales Situation

A car salesman, faced with the objection that a competitive model has more inside room, might say: "When you say that the Blastoff station wagon has more cubic feet inside, let's look at in terms of usable space, not just cubic feet. This might not have occurred to you in making that comparison, so let's look at the design of our wagon in terms of space that can be actually used to carry things. . ."

When a purchasing agent tries to dismiss a salesman purely on the basis of his company's higher price, the salesman might bridge with this type of approach: "You're saying that our price is higher based solely on the difference in the cost per unit. Naturally, you haven't had an opportunity to study the other costs that are involved in putting an assembly such as ours into a finished product. This brings into play a lot of other costs over and beyond the unit price you pay us. Now, here are some of the other factors which will make our product cost less by the time you have installed it in your finished product. . ."

The Supervisory Situation

Young people in management frequently express impractical ideas, yet to preserve their motivation, their superiors do not want to be too blunt in discouraging them. An executive might say to a management trainee: "I can see you're devoting a lot of thought to new and different ideas which might help the company (an "I" technique which follows). "When you do come on an idea, test it out to see what effect it has on other departments. Now in this case, your idea might have this effect on the Sales Department." By "thinking it through" with the trainee, he removes blame.

When someone opposes a policy of the company, a supervisor might use this technique by saying: "Now let's see why it is that the company set that policy. First,. . ."

When a person finds fault with some aspect of company benefits, this technique works well because his supervisor can help him "think through" to the effect that that particular benefit has on others with different family circumstances.

The Family And Personal Situation

This technique becomes very useful for parents in handling young people who are going through the stage called "adolescent rebellion." They object to the disciplines imposed on them by educators, elders—even the police. Parents can "think through" with them the consequences that would result from a lack of rules, laws, social disciplines, ethics, or morals. In the process, they may be able to demonstrate that each person relinquishes some freedom in return for the benefits derived from social living.

A typical example of how this technique might work could involve a father and his son. His son has a traffic violation for running a "yellow" light and protests that it was at night and there was no traffic, etc. The father "thinks it through" by pointing out that if everyone ran "yellow" lights there would ultimately be a serious accident and that each person must respect the law without expecting special conditions to provide exemption for him. The fact that he "thinks it through" with his son removes the blame for the wrong attitude.

If the "crowd" wants to go to a drive-in movie, but you want to stay home and watch television, blame will be removed if you work gradually around to the idea that we can have drinks at home while we watch television. "Well, I wouldn't mind going to the drive-in, but then let's stop and think about some of the things we can do at home that we can't do if we go. Like, for one thing, we can't have a drink if we go out to the drive-in."

BR-7   Re-state His "Wrong" Idea Nearer To Your Position

Many times we can remove blame for a wrong idea or attitude by the use of a different word or phrase to bring the idea closer to the one we want. When we re-state the idea in a "translated" form we can effectively change it.

An interesting example occurred when a union was trying to organize a company with whom I was doing consulting work. The union was making a great point of the higher wages paid by a similar type of company in a nearby city. The supervision effectively changed the opinion of enough workers to vote down the union effort, using this BR-7 technique. Each time an employee brought up the subject of wages, he would express it in terms of hourly rates. Each supervisor was trained to change the phraseology to "annual income." "You talk about wages per hour. The important thing is annual income. The 15¢ additional per hour that you're talking about won't pay rent or buy groceries. Why? Because every one of our employees had year-round employment last year. The plants your're talking about had three layoffs amounting to a total of ten weeks per employee. So their annual income figures out to be better than 15% less than ours, even with the lower hourly rate we pay."

This technique can be employed with great effectiveness wherever it becomes possible to make a re-statement that reverses the "wrong" attitude or objection.

The Sales Situation

Suppose a prospect for an automobile says that a neighbor has told him that your deluxe model with the "big" engine and automatic transmission is a "gas eater." As a car salesman you could reply: "What your neighbor is saying is that our 325-horsepower engine and automatic transmission lowered his gasoline mileage when compared with a smaller engine and a clutch-type shift. The question is 'How much lower?' The figures show that with normal driving and care in starting up from a dead stop, the difference can be as little as one to two miles per gallon. What's more important, then, is how much comfort and safety does the big engine offer you for the few cents it costs in each tank of gasoline."

Frequently those who voice a negative opinion will use strong words (such as "gas eater"). When these words are changed to more precise and accurate language, the negative attitude may be opposed and blame has been removed. I heard a salesman answer the objection to "all that chrome plate" on a deluxe automobile, by referring to the chromium plating as "protective metallic strips." He showed that they were not just decorative, but that they were placed at points at which slight scraping abrasions would remove the paint!

An objection to "high price" can be changed to "high quality" and the word "costly" can be changed to "higher value." In each case, the change in wording removes the blame by giving the other person a "new" phrase or expression to substitute.

The Supervisory Situation

We have already shown how criticisms about "wages" can be

"translated" to annual income for a supervisor who is faced with that objection.

In another situation, a supervisor was told by one of his subordinates that "Charlie is your teacher's pet. He gets all the overtime." This overstatement was re-phrased to refer to Charlie as "the man who was most available and never refused to work overtime" and "all" was changed to "that's why he gets a little more overtime than the rest of the fellows."

A chief executive, tired of hearing his vice president for sales speak derogatorily about engineers (he called them "those damn drawing board weasels"), translated the phrase to "men with training· in exact methods" and showed the need that the business had for men who could produce exact data.

A young executive who was talking with me in a counselling interview referred to the chief executive as an "old fogey." I changed this: "Charley is advanced in years, although he won't be 65 for three years. But as we get older we do get more set in our ways. However, I have never found Mr. Snodgrass unreasonable if handled with tact and skill."

The Family And Personal Situation

This technique is very important in family and social situations. Why? Because in the intimate relations that we find there, each person is prone to overstatement and each of us is prone to counter with an overstatement. That always starts an argument. If we re-phrase an overstatement closer to our position, we prevent an argument and remove blame.

A wife says: "I don't care if Jack Jones is a good customer of yours, his wife is a boresome busybody and I'm not going out to dinner with them."

Your reply: "Perhaps the reason Mrs. Jones talks about people so much and so often is that she doesn't know anything else to talk about. Her education is limited. Why don't you try getting her interested in the work you do for the Art Association?"

A child who has been reproved for bad behavior screams: "You don't love me!"

This is changed to: "We don't want you to make mistakes and get into trouble, but that's because we do love you."

To Get The Most Out Of This Chapter

We have completed the first two letters of our "BRIDGE" by showing how to use blame removers. The fine thing about blame removers is that they can frequently be combined with other techniques such as the ones which will follow in later chapters. It is always a good idea to use a blame remover even when we follow it with some other technique. It adds power to our effectiveness in dealing with wrong ideas, wrong attitudes, or objections.

As you did in previous chapters dealing with techniques in presenting ideas, write down the seven types of blame removers.

Then think of an example from your home, personal or business life. If you are a salesman, think of real objections that might come from a customer.

Select "Key" Phrases

There are many "key" phrases which can be used in connection with each of the blame removers. Look at the ones which follow and then think of additional ones that apply to your own life situations.

BR-1   (Many People Agree With The "Wrong" Idea)

"I've heard a lot of people say that. . ."
"Most people get that idea at first. . ."
"You'd be surprised how often people say that to me. . ."

BR-2   (Blame Yourself For The "Wrong" Idea)

"I'm sorry I gave you the wrong impression. . ."
"I must have neglected to point out. . ."
"Perhaps I didn't make this point clear. . ."

BR-3   (It Was Natural And Logical)

"I can see why you would feel that way. . ."
"People with your training naturally get that idea. . ."
"You feel that way because of the way you were treated. . ."

BR-4   (Agree, But Show That Others Will Not)

"It looks the same way to me, however. . ."
"I'm like you, I can't see why it should be that way, but. . ."
"Being a layman, too, I can't quite understand that, yet. . ."

BR-5   (You Felt The Same Way Until You Learned Better)

"That's how it looked to me until. . ."
"I thought the same thing, but they showed me. . ."
"Before I studied the situation I thought that, too. . ."

BR-6   (He Has Not Had A Chance To "Think It Through")

"Off the cuff, it looks that way, but there are other factors. . ."
"At first blush one would think that way. . ."
"Before you look below the surface, you tend to feel as you do. . ."

BR-7   (Re-State The "Wrong" Idea)

To do this exercise take several negative words that you have heard others use and find a word that "softens" or alters that strong statement. Someone says he "hates" a person and you say: "The reason he doesn't appeal to you. . ." Someone says, "It's a fraud" and you change this to: "The reason this appears wrong to you. . ."

A very good idea is to memorize these phrases for use in blame removing, including the ones shown here and the three or four that you should be able to create.

Soon you'll find that blame removing is a real tool for power in opposing wrong ideas, negative attitudes, or objections to your ideas!

Special Note To Sales Supervisors

The BR techniques can provide excellent sales training sessions. Use "role-playing" by letting one salesman state an objection to a product or feature, then call on another salesman to use one of the BR techniques before opposing it.

Chapter Eight

INFLATE
HIS IMPORTANCE
BEFORE YOU OPPOSE HIM

The next important letter-symbol in our key word "BRIDGE" is the letter "I." This could stand for three words, all having to do with the power to oppose negative ideas or attitudes and all beginning with an "I."

"I" stands for the fact that we inflate his personal worth before opposing his idea. It also stands for the fact that we build up his importance, the same thing. It might also stand for the word "introduction" because this is an introductory "bridge" between his expression of the negative position and your opposition to it.

Just as the blame removers provided an anaesthetic to precede the psychological surgery of removing the wrong idea, so the "I" techniques have the effect of palliating any pain involved in giving up the idea you oppose.

"I" Techniques May Combine With BR Techniques

Those who show great power in opposing wrong ideas or

attitudes frequently combine "I" techniques with blame removers.

For example, in our BR-3 techniques we showed that it was "natural" and "logical" for the other person to have the wrong idea. This removed blame. At the same time, however, the "natural and logical" reason was a compliment. The mother who said that it was natural and logical for a popular girl like her daughter to want to accept all dates, even on school nights, was combining a build-up with a blame remover. The same could be true of some of the self-blaming techniques. When we blame ourselves for the wrong idea held by the other person, we are building him up by diminishing our own personal worth.

Five "I" Techniques

There are five techniques which fit the "I" classification. Some of them are similar to the "B" techniques (build-up) that we used to present ideas. Some of the principles involved are almost identical, while others are quite different because we are opposing ideas instead of presenting them.

I-1   Praise the person for his understanding or open-mindedness.

I-2   Show that many qualified or worthy people agree with the "wrong" idea.

I-3   Express modesty or humility before opposing.

I-4   Appear embarrassed by the "wrong" idea.

I-5   Concede a point before opposing the "wrong" idea.

Let's look at these five techniques and show examples of how they work to provide a "bridge" by inflating and increasing importance.

I-1   Praise The Person For His Understanding Or Open-Mindedness

In using this technique we must have some real evidence of the other person's understanding or open-mindedness. As we showed in discussing B-2 in Chapter Five, flattery is damaging to personal worth because it implies the person is susceptible to flattery. Where we do have some evidence of understanding or open-mindedness, I-1 is very useful.

The Sales Situation

A Purchasing Agent who is refusing to make a purchase because of a price differential might find that the salesman could successfully oppose him by saying: "I know that you always keep up to date on modern purchasing techniques and I've heard you speak on value analysis. For that reason, I think you will agree with me that the slight price differential is more than offset by the ways in which our products fit so neatly into your assembly procedures. . ."

A prospect for an automobile has quoted a neighbor as critical of this salesman's car's automatic transmission, but has added: "Of course, that's just one man's opinion."

The salesman them comes back, "I can see that while you listened to your neighbor you want to find out the facts for yourself. That's always wise in making a purchase as important as a new automobile. So let's get down to the actual mechanics of our transmission and see why it gains such good acceptance."

The Supervisory Situation

A supervisor says to a workman: "When we talked last week about that grievance that had been filed in Department 12, you said: 'I think the Union is wrong on that one.' That means that you think for yourself and can see both sides of these issues between management and employees. Now the reason for the second-shift differential is this. . ."

Chief Executive to Sales Executive (who has complained of a product design weakness): "We had that same situation two years ago and you were quick to tell your boys that we'd have to live with it until we moved that year's inventory. Now we have the same situation and I know you'll be willing to do your best until we can make the change."

The Family and Personal Situation

A father says to his son (who has complained about a traffic ticket): "When Charles lost his license for that third speeding violation you said there were sure two sides to it and that

Charles was known for his tendency to drive too fast. That shows that you recognize that the traffic officers have their problems. Now, in this case, consider the fact that the officer can't make a special concession to you."

A teacher says to a student who complains about a heavy assignment: "You were nice enough to say that the assignment two weeks ago only took thirty minutes of your study time and made it possible for you to catch up on your history. So while this assignment is a little longer than usual, I think you can see why we have to move a little faster for this week."

Many times the praise for open-mindedness and understanding can stem from knowledge of the person's occupation, background, or training. "As a lawyer you know there are always two sides to a question." "As an accountant you want to see something like this in black and white." "As an engineer you are used to getting exact data before proceeding." In each case this is followed by the specific information to dispel the wrong idea or attitude.

I-2   Show That Many Qualified Or Worthy People Agree With The "Wrong" Idea

In BR-1 we removed blame by showing that *many* people had the same wrong idea or attitude. This proves especially useful for commonly-held misconceptions. The fact that the concept was common to many people removed the blame, but did not increase importance.

So, BR-1 emphasized the removing of blame. I-2 emphasizes the quality of the people who agree with the "wrong" idea or attitude and thus identifies the person with people of quality. We build up the importance of the other person—we inflate his sense of personal worth—by showing that he is traveling in good company even though we later show that he is wrong.

The Sales Situation

An automobile prospect has objected to the new system of braking installed in a new model. The salesman says: "In the last month I've talked to three graduate engineers who brought up the same question about our new brake system. When I explained the figures we obtained from the proving ground tests at both high and low speeds, they could see that this was a better way to brake the car and that it would be less expensive in the long run."

A purchasing agent has questioned a new design for a control assembly. The salesman says: "When you raise that question you're joining a very distinguished group of buyers. Two of our largest customers wouldn't believe the new control would stand up as well as the old one, so we gave them some production samples to put through their testing labs. After the tests we got big orders from both of them. Now, you don't have a lab like they have, but you are concerned about the same factors, so here's what they say from their lab findings. . ."

A wholesale salesman might say: "Some of our best dealers felt the same way. . ." Other phrases could include: "Some of the most experienced people feel that way. . .", "The smartest purchasing agents always raise that question. . .", or, "A man who has owned four of our deluxe models objected to that until I showed him."

The Supervisory Situation

An executive might say to a management trainee: "Some of our best management trainees objected to their period of field training."

A chief executive might say to a subordinate: "In my years of watching promising men come up to the top, I've had to argue that point with all of them. But when they saw. . ."

A design engineer who is impatient to see a new idea incorporated into a product might be handled in this way: "The men who are best motivated for design work are always eager to see their work incorporated into the product. I don't blame them, but the economics of things requires that we get the investment out of our tools before we make a change."

The Family or Personal Situation

A professor might say to a student who objects to "grading on the curve": "You know a lot of the students who are on the

Dean's Honor Roll feel the same way. However, let me show you why it is the fairest way to grade."

A father might say to a son: "You know, the boys who are actually the most skillful drivers are inclined to take more chances, thinking that they can always squeak out of it, but then comes the time. . ."

Remember the BR-3 in which the mother praised her daughter because she was popular, then showed that it was natural and logical for her to feel that way?

I-3   Express Modesty Or Humility Before Opposing

This technique is much the same as the B-1 way of presenting an idea by diminishing our own personal worth, the "teeter-totter" principle. When your personal worth is reduced, the other person's rises.

Now we employ this same principle to oppose a "wrong" idea or negative attitude. In the face-to-face situation we make him feel bigger, more important, and thus ready to give up his idea.

The Sales Situation

An automobile prospect has questioned the stability of a new steering mechanism at high speeds. The salesman replies: "I do very little high-speed or turnpike driving, so I don't have the experience that you have. However, several traveling salesmen who use their cars at high speeds have reported that this gives them better control at high speeds."

An insurance prospect has objected to life insurance as a "needless expense." The insurance salesman replies: "My wife and I aren't lucky enough to have any children and I sure envy you those fine young ones. If I were lucky enough to have a pair of fine children, I'd think of insurance as an investment for them instead of an expense."

A female office manager has to talk to one of the younger girls about her attire, which is too "revealing." She says: "At my age I know that men aren't going to give me a second look so I dress conservatively. But we want the customers who come in to keep their mind on our products, so. . ."

The treasurer is talking to the sales executive who has complained about the detailed requirements of the expense account form which his men have to fill out. The Treasurer says: "I don't travel very much and I don't do any company entertaining. Wish my job called for more of that. As a result, I don't know much about entertaining costs. However, I think the boys should know that if the Income Tax people should audit them they might have to account for their expense claims."

The Family or Personal Situation

A father might say to a son whose grades are "down": "I realize that everything has changed and that there is a 'generation gap.' There's so much more for young people to learn and do these days. I'm glad I didn't have to face your situation. But one thing hasn't changed: You have to make grades or you can't finish your education."

A husband might say to his wife: "I don't know anything about menu planning and you're the one who studies gourmet cooking and all that kind of thing. What I'm saying is that the men nearly always order beef when they go out to dinner."

I-4   Appear Embarrassed By The "Wrong" Idea

This is another means to diminish your own personal worth before you oppose the "wrong" idea or attitude. As a result, you have built up his personal worth. He has really "floored you" or made it difficult to create a meaningful answer.

This might be "acting" or it might be "real." It gives you an opportunity to be honest and frank if the wrong idea or objection does "stump you." If you're a good "actor" you might use it as a good "bridge" even when you have a ready answer.

In some cases this may overlap with the "delaying" techniques which will be discussed later. The expressions of embarrassment may provide some cushion of time. The main purpose, however, is to build the other person up by dignifying his objection or his "wrong" idea.

The Sales Situation

When an automobile prospect says that he has been offered a very (perhaps ridiculously) high trade-in offer by a competitor, the salesman may use this technique. "Gee, that is *some* price for your present car! I don't know how they can do it. It sure leaves me in a hole. But let's see how far apart we are (gets out pencil) and maybe we can talk to our used car manager and see where we stand. He may have some ideas."

A purchasing agent raises a question about liability claims in case a purchased control causes failure of their finished product. The salesman says: "You know that's the first time anybody has brought that up, so I'm somewhat at a loss for an answer. However, we're one of the largest manufacturers in the field and I am going to presume that we'll be carrying product liability insurance to take care of such contingencies."

The Supervisory Situation

A workman has protested the method of sampling used to establish work standards and has raised a question involving higher mathematics. The supervisor says: "You've got me there. Obviously, you know something about math and statistics that I don't know. It would take a methods engineer to answer that question. However, from a practical standpoint, the standards they have set have turned out to be fair down through the years that I've been supervising."

A chief executive finds that two of his subordinates are at odds over a matter of policy. One of them expresses his position so strongly that the Chief is actually embarrassed. "Wow! I didn't realize that things had gone that far. I should have been keeping better track of how you two were getting along on that matter. Maybe I've been away from the office too much. I hope it's not too late to get some kind of agreement. Now let's see what your position is and how far apart you and Charlie are."

The Family or Personal Situation

A daughter has said: "After all, I'm eighteen and I could run off and get married if I wanted to, so I don't see why I have to be in by 1:00 o'clock."

Her mother says: "I just don't know how to answer that one, dear. I had no idea you felt that strongly about a matter that your dad and I feel is just good parenthood. You frighten me a little by what you say. Now let's reason this out."

In a political discussion, a man has objected to your candidate by saying that "all politicians are crooks." You are shocked and you show it. Then you proceed to prove that your candidate has an excellent record for honesty. However, you should combine this with a blame remover to excuse him for having made such a strong statement.

I-5 Concede A Point Before Opposing The Other Person

This is the tool described by many sales trainers as the "yes, but. . ." technique. It has been mentioned for years by inspirational speakers who talk to sales groups. The result is that many young salesmen overwork the technique. Many of them sound like a broken record and their over-use of the words "yes. . . but" carries no meaning. I heard a life insurance salesman use the words, "Yes, but," some fifteen times in as many minutes.

This is one of the reasons for careful study of all of the techniques discussed in this and the preceding and following chapters. Over-use of any one technique creates a triteness and monotony that hurts your power to deal with people.

Nevertheless, this is a powerful technique when used skillfully and with some originality. It is an effective bridge and it does build up the other person's feeling of importance and inflate his personal worth when properly used.

The Sales Situation

An insurance prospect has said: "All you'll do is invest my money and charge me for administering it. I might as well put several hundred dollars a year into investments myself."

The salesman agrees, in part: "You're right. If you put the same amount into investments as you pay us in premiums you would probably have the money to put your children through college by the time they reached that age. The reason for buying insurance is to guarantee they'll be able to go to college even if you lose your life or become totally disabled and lose your income."

We can go back to the car prospect who objects to the gasoline used in an automobile with an automatic transmission. The car salesman concedes the point, in part: "Yes, you're right when you say that automatic transmissions use more gas for the typical driver. However, many drivers are able to have the convenience of an automatic transmission with no great increase in gasoline consumption. The difference is negligible in such cases because they let the car reach its normal speed gradually. While this is true of all automatic transmissions, let me show you why ours has the greatest advantage in gasoline consumption."

The Supervisory Situation

The workman who objects to safety shoes because they are hotter and heavier gets a concession from his foreman: "Sure, I agree with you and I don't blame you for objecting to the fact that safety shoes are hotter and heavier than ordinary shoes. But remember, they're a lot less uncomfortable than a broken instep, crushed foot, or amputated toe!"

We could use this technique in the situation involving hourly wages and annual income that we used in BR-7. When the workman complains that the hourly rates at ABC Manufacturing Company are higher, the foreman concedes it. "Sure, their hourly rates are higher than ours—about 5% more, on the average. But we haven't had a layoff in three years and they'll average about five weeks a year. That more than offsets the difference in take-home pay. That's 10% less for the whole year."

The Personal and Family Situation

Differences of opinion in social situations can often be resolved amicably by an I-5 concession. I heard a gin rummy player (four-handed game) criticize his partner: "If you had gone down and let him undercut you, we'd have still saved the 'box.' "

His partner replied: "You're right and I should have played it that way. But you could see his hand and I couldn't. I figured he was holding two cards to play on me and that way he couldn't gin."

When a teenager complained to his father that "cops are always trying to get something on us kids and let older folks get by with traffic violations that they stick us for," the father replied: "Yes, I imagine that the traffic policemen do keep a more careful eye on young drivers than on older people. You see, son, most of the accidents are being caused by younger people and the police want to prevent accidents."

To Get The Most Out Of This Chapter

When it is necessary to oppose a "wrong" idea, a negative attitude or an objection to something you want to get acceptance for, there are these five "I" ways in which we can increase personal worth and importance. "I" stands for "inflate" or "importance" and fits into our BRIDGE which makes it easier to oppose negative expressions or attitudes.

They may be used by themselves under some circumstances, but they can also follow or precede some of the blame removers to add more Power to your ability to oppose negative ideas or attitudes.

Take a piece of notepaper and try to write down the five "I" techniques. If you can't remember one or two of them, look them up—but then write them down!

Now write out an example for each of the five for each of three situations: Sales, Supervisor, or Family-Social. You should end up with fifteen examples.

Special Note For Sales Supervisors

As with the BR techniques, you can use "role-playing" sales meetings to give your men practice in meeting objections. Set up a series of customer objections and have each of your men use one of the "I" techniques to bridge his statements to offset the objection.

Chapter Nine

HOW TO
USE "DELAY" IN OPPOSING
NEGATIVE IDEAS

In working with sales training groups the word "stalling" frequently comes up. Good salesmen recognize that when a customer expresses an objection that is difficult to answer, the best thing to do is to "stall" while you get ready to present your opposing viewpoint. There is sound thinking in this approach. However, there is more basic psychology involved than just gaining time. The "Delay" or "D" techniques in our BRIDGE produce additional benefits, as we will see.

In the dynamics of a face-to-face situation, we not only gain time by using a "D" technique, but the fact that we place a "cushion" of time between his expression and our opposition has the effect of preserving his personal worth. The immediate rejoinder may stimulate a counter-statement that exaggerates the opposition. In some cases, where a strong statement has been made by the other person, it gives him time to feel a pang of regret that he made an overstatement originally.

As we will see, the Delay may be quite short as in D-1 and it may be fairly lengthy if we use D-2 or D-4.

The principle to keep in mind is: "If you cushion your disagreement it may serve as a protection to the other person's feeling of personal worth."

THE "DELAY" TECHNIQUES—FOUR IN NUMBER

D-1 Show that the "wrong" idea involves a matter of taste or choice; reduce its importance.

D-2 Appear to study the objection very carefully.

D-3 Make the "wrong" idea or objection seem unimportant in the total scheme of things, the "big" picture.

D-4 Change the subject; break the continuity.

D-1   Show That The "Wrong" Idea Involves A Matter Of Taste Or Choice; Reduce Its Importance

Here the delay involves the mentioning of alternative choices other than the "wrong" one, finally returning to your own idea as the best solution. Sometimes the technique may include an actual "inventory" of other choices, in other cases it may simply involve the statement that there are other (or that there are many) choices.

The Sales Situation

A purchasing agent for thermostats (to be put into their furnaces) has raised an objection to the design of the salesman's thermostat. The salesman replies, "Of course there are a lot of different approaches to thermostat design. Each has some differences and some features that are patentable. Some are more expensive than ours, others cheaper. Now we feel that our particular design fits better into your production procedures and your particular furnace design."

An automobile prospect has raised a question about the type of wheel suspension and springing in this salesman's car. He replies, "As you know, the automobile industry has experimented with a lot of different types of wheel suspension and springing. You have studied the arguments put forth by Blastoff Motors for their particular type of suspension and springing. Our engineers don't agree with their method for several reasons. For one thing, our engineers have developed our suspension to permit you to brake to a smooth stop without any 'diving' sensation as the brakes are applied. The front end does not 'dip.' Let's take a ride in my demonstrator and I'll show you how it works." This same technique can be used for a wide variety of product features—automatic transmissions, steering, etc.

The Supervisory Situation

Again we use the example of a workman who complains to his foreman about the setting of work standards. The foreman says, "Well, you know there are a lot of different methods used by engineers and time study men to set standards. Some companies use purely analytical methods like Methods Time Measurement while others study workmen with a stop watch. Some of them use moving pictures or video tape. I've worked with standards that have been set by all of these different methods and it has been my observation that there is very little difference in the final outcome. In this case. . ."

A management trainee has raised an objection to the training program which requires him to be assigned to work in a production department for a period of time. His supervisor tells him, "Well, that's one of the features of our training program that was put into effect by our training director. He has studied all of the different ways in which companies handle college trainees like yourself. He says that some of them have very formal training programs involving mostly classroom work. Others have them 'visit around' to various administrative departments, while others assign them to production departments like we do. However, our production assignments are very short and here are some of the advantages our system provides you. . ."

The Family or Personal Situation

The mother whose daughter objects to the rules her parent have set for dating and curfew times, may reply: "I suppose different parents take a different approach to what they expect of their daughters when they start dating. I know that some of them are much more rigid than your father and I are. I've heard them discuss the matter. Now you claim that Mary and Sue have much more liberal rules than the ones we expect of you. That doesn't prove that we're wrong and it doesn't mean that we're unfair."

In a political discussion another person prefers his candidate because "he makes such a good appearance." You come back with: "People vote for candidates for a lot of different reasons. Appearance is one of them. Some people vote for the man with the best record, others because they happen to know him personally, and so on. The reason I'm for Senator Jones has to do with his stand on issues that are important to all of us in business."

D-2 Appear To Study The Objection Very Carefully

We not only achieve delay if we study an objection very carefully, but we also elevate the other person's sense of personal worth because we are giving careful consideration to his objection or negative attitude.

Sometimes it is very desirable to have a pencil and paper handy so that you can jot down the "evidence" on both sides of the case. This adds a visual stimulus which may help to put the point across. This is demonstrated in our first example.

The Sales Situation

The car prospect says that you are $50.00 higher than a competitor. The salesman says, "Now you say that we're $50.00 higher than Downtown Blastoff Motors because they appraised your car at $2,000 instead of $1,950. First we ought to check to be sure we're talking about the same model with the same features and extras. Let's check them off." He does this. "Now do you have their working figures?" Prospect doesn't have them. "Well, did you notice if there was a calculation for sales tax at the bottom of the sheet?" Prospect doesn't think so.

"Well our management always requires that we include the sales tax in a competitive 'deal' and we have done that. That involves a $60.00 difference right there and makes us $10.00 cheaper, even without taking into account the plus factors that we have in our car."

An unusual application of D-2 involves a sales engineer who told me that when he ran into a difficult objection he always pulled out his pocket slide rule. While he mumbles to himself, he works the slide rule and sometimes makes notes on a pad. Then he says something like this: "Well, there are a lot of variables involved, but I still feel our solution to your problem is the better one. Let me show you why." The humorous side of this man's approach is that he doesn't actually figure anything with the slide rule. It simply gives him some time—a "delay." In this delaying time he is planning how to shape his opposition to the objection!

The Supervisory Situation

A workman has claimed that the foreman's reprimand violates his rights under the union contract. The foreman says (with full knowledge that he is right), "Well, let's see what the contract actually says. I've got a copy right in my desk drawer. I think that comes under Section 6 where it deals with absenteeism and proper notice, but we ought to look to be sure."

The sales manager has asked to buy some advertising and the chief executive feels it would not be a profitable investment. Instead of challenging the wisdom of the purchase, he says, "Well, let's look at the budget." He calls for the budget figures and as they go over the budgeted items, he shows that they would have to change some other planned expenditure in order to do what the sales manager wants to do.

The Family or Personal Situation

A father is having a problem with his son who wants to go to a very expensive university instead of the less-costly nearby state university. The son says that he can't get the course work he wants at the state university. Father says, "Well, we have both catalogs here. Let's look at the State curriculum and see what they have in the field you want to study." Father is able to prove his point, but the D-2 technique made it seem less blunt or assertive.

The "crowd" is having a slight difference of opinion about where to go out for dinner. Three of them want to go to an Italian eating place, but one person is holding out because he wants a "thick steak." You say, "Well, let's find out. Maybe Antonio has some good steaks. Sometimes he does. Why don't we call him up?" So the call is placed and they find out that Antonio has a "very good T-bone. Nice and thick." So the D-2 technique has worked and everybody is happy.

D-3 Make The "Wrong" Idea Seem Unimportant In The Total Scheme Or The "Big" Picture

This method is limited to those situations in which the negative attitude or "wrong" idea is actually unimportant. It is different in this respect from D-1 where we make the idea seem unimportant by showing one or more alternatives that are just as good. It is a "D" technique, when properly used, because the words used to describe the lack of importance offer a "cushion" between the expression and your opposition.

One thing to keep in mind with D-3 is that it is particularly useful for alarmists who tend to "make a mountain out of a molehill." If we do not protect their personal worth the mountain will continue to grow larger. This is their nature. The use of clichés such as, "Well, a hundred years from now it won't make any difference" actually makes an assault on the alarmist's feeling of personal worth. Such trite phrases will tend to aggravate the situation.

The Sales Situation

A salesman who is faced with the objection that his trade-in offer is $50 lower than a competitor's may sometimes find D-3 useful. "I don't blame you for wanting to try to get $50 additional for your car (blame remover). After all $50 is $50. However, remember that we're talking about a $4,000 automobile and that only amounts to a little more than 1% of the investment you're making. Then, too, records show that our cars actually have a higher trade-in value after two or three years than the car you are trading in. You will probably get more than your $50 back when you buy your next car." He then proceeds to recapitulate all of the values, competitively, that he has previously pointed out in his presentation.

For another example we can refer back to the situation in Chapter Three in which the millionaire refrigerator prospect could see that odds of seven to six were small when he could buy the "Yankees" of the refrigerator business. When the difference was $100 it seemed large; when reduced to gambling odds, it became unimportant. Of course, it was the "magic multiplier" that closed that sale, but the D-2 technique was the clincher.

The Supervisory Situation

A management trainee has made a blunder and goes to the personnel director. He feels his future has been placed in jeopardy and wants to transfer. "Don't let that worry you. I know Joe, your boss, and he is very understanding. He knows you just started with us last June. He isn't the kind of person that will let this affect your annual review. Look at it this way. . ."

Manager to supervisor who is "shook-up" because his department has shown a set-back in the past week. "Look, if you're going to let things like that upset you, you're going to be in a 'dither' all of the time. We expect periods in which turnover gets high in a department like yours. Think of it this way: A supervisor's job is to solve problems. You should welcome dilemmas like this one because it gives you a chance to show that you can lick a problem. . ."

The Personal or Family Situation

The husband whose wife has objected to wearing her "blue

satin" to the Johnsons' party, might say, "Well, let's start counting noses. I can't think of anyone who will be at the Johnsons' party who was at the Country Club formal last spring. Anyway, if they were there we weren't in the same group with them. You're the only one who'll be at the Johnsons' who'll know it isn't new!"

The first time our son and one of his close friends "gypped" school to go follow an exhibition golf match, the mother of his friend called me (because I'm a "psychologist") and wanted to know what to do about it. She had plans for all kinds of punishment that were far too severe. I said, "Well, let's think that one over. First of all these boys, both of them, have a record of excellent deportment and good grades. Sometimes I think they're a little too 'good.' I'm a little glad that they asserted their independence, but I don't mean that we should just overlook it. Let's talk to the principal and see what his plans are before we do anything ourselves. Maybe he'll be doing enough to make them see they shouldn't have 'gypped.' "

D-4 Change The Subject or Break The Continuity

The big difference between D-4 and the other D techniques is that D-4 is a frank and open delay or interruption. We don't disclose our reason for the delay or indicate that we are trying to "cushion" our subsequent opposition. However, it is obvious in D-4 that we are making a break between the discussion and the disagreement. Usually it is obvious that we intend to come back to the subject and the disagreement, but the delay is obvious and sometimes evidently deliberate.

If we change the subject we should do it with good tact and good "manners." Frequently, if we know the other person well enough, the change of subject may be toward something in which he has a personal interest. The baseball fan will not object if we interrupt by saying, "By the way, didn't those Mets surprise you?"

The Sales Situation

A skillful salesman told me this story: When he called on the purchasing agent, he was irate and flatly said he was going to change suppliers. "You missed that last delivery date and we had to shut down one of our assembly lines. I'm looking for another source right now."

The salesman was able to get a two-hour interruption by saying, "Yes, that was a bad situation. I didn't realize that it caused you to have to shut down. That's expensive. Let me ask a small favor of you. Before you commit yourself to changing suppliers, let me call the home office (he looked at his watch)—it will have to be after lunch. Let me get all the facts about how the misunderstanding took place. Since it has never happened before, there may be some reason for it that neither of us knows about. I'll get the call in and see you again some time between 1:30 and 2:00." After lunch the purchasing agent had "calmed down." He was in a mood to listen to reason. The problem lay in a typographical error in the date on the requisition form. The fault was with the buyer, not the seller! Without the D-4 technique, the salesman might have lost a valuable customer.

A car salesman told me how he handled a customer who flatly stated that he would buy the car only if he could get delivery in three weeks (to the day). The salesman knew that this could not be done. If he said so, the prospect would have to stand by his threat and refuse to buy. The salesman said, "By the way, we have coffee and cokes in our customer lounge over by the service department. How about a cup of coffee?" They went for the coffee and sat comfortably while the salesman reviewed the features of the car. Eventually the man came out with the reason for the three-week ultimatum. It was a birthday present for his wife. The salesman then proposed that they get a color picture of the new car and a gift certificate and use that for the birthday present. The story had a happy ending because the salesman used a D-4 technique.

The Supervisory Situation

A general manager used this technique very effectively. He called in his three prime subordinates to propose a new program to them. All three of them objected violently and instantly. They found things wrong from the production, finance, and sales points of view. He looked at the clock. "I haven't had my mid-morning coffee. How about you fellows? Let's slip over to the hotel and get a cup." They did. Twenty minutes later he was back with them in his office. "I can see that my idea went over like a lead ballon with you guys. But give me a chance to point out some other angles." The delay took the "heat" out of the situation.

A supervisor who was getting a heated protest from a workman, with the workman threatening to file a grievance, looked at his watch and said: "Excuse me. . .I've got to see the boss in five minutes. I'll be back with you after the conference is finished." Thirty minutes later the workman had "cooled down" and they were able to settle the difference of opinion.

The Family or Personal Situation

My wife and I have found that the D-4 technique has had a very beneficial effect on our marriage. Years ago we developed the practice of terminating a discussion when we could not agree. "Let's talk about it tomorrow." When tomorrow came the difference was not nearly so great and no argument took place! It took us a few years to learn that. Perhaps you can learn it now.

In a heated political argument, I overheard a lawyer who was very skilled in dealing with people say: "Well, we've had a few drinks and neither of us has access to the facts that we're arguing about. I have some files at the office to show how Senator Jones has voted and if you'll meet me for lunch at the club, I'll bring them along." He got the campaign contribution that he was seeking at lunch the next day!

To Get The Most Out Of This Chapter

We have discussed four techniques which help to make a "bridge" of "delay" between a "wrong" idea, attitude or negative position and our subsequent effort to overcome it.

They involve the exploration of alternatives, the apparent deep study of the situation, making the matter seem unimportant or less important and simply creating a "break" in the discussion.

While not universally useful—they won't work in every case—they are important to the person who would develop power to deal with people. They are especially useful, in possible combination with other techniques, where the opposing idea is actually not extremely important or where some interruption is needed to allow a "cooling off" period.

As in Chapter Eight, take a piece of paper and write down the codes D-1, D-2, D-3, and D-4 and then try to remember what each stands for. If you can't remember—look them up—but be sure to write them down to help you remember.

Then think of an example of each one in a situation with which you are familiar. Think of an example for a sales situation, an office or business situation, and a personal or family situation. You should have twelve examples, three for each of the four "D" techniques.

Special Note For Sales Supervisors

As in earlier chapters, you can build a sales meeting around the "D" techniques, using each of them in order and discussing them with your men before asking for examples. "Role-playing" can be employed using typical expressions of customer opposition or objections. Get each of your men to show how he might use each of the four techniques.

Chapter Ten

USING
"FORCING" TECHNIQUES IN
OPPOSING IDEAS

When we used the word "BRIDGE" as an acronym to help remember the different techniques of opposing negative attitudes or ideas, our last two letters were GE. We said that these were the techniques in which we would "Get Embarrassing" or create embarrassment for the individual if he did not relinquish his idea or opposition. We also said that GE could stand for "Go Easy" because these techniques may be dangerous. They may cause arguments to start. They should be used as a last resort or under special circumstances when we can be sure they have a good chance to work.

No One Likes "Force" In Face-to-Face Situations

No one likes to be forced to change his position. There is a resistance to anything that sounds like a threat. Yet we cannot overlook these "GE" techniques because there are times when they become effective after everything else has failed. There are times when the very nature of the idea we are opposing suggests a need for these forcing methods. There are times, too, when the bantering nature of GE-2 may provide a humorous let-down in a difficult face-to-face situation.

As we will show, each of the techniques has its own special usefulness in special situations. As a result, we must include them if we are to show how to develop power in overcoming ideas and attitudes that block our goals.

Related To Techniques In Chapter Six

There is a relationship between these "GE" techniques and the "L" and "D" techniques of getting acceptance for an idea as discussed in Chapter Six. We showed that a person could suffer a loss of personal worth by not accepting an idea ("L") and that we might use "reverse English" and get him to disagree (D) with the opposite of our idea. The same warnings expressed in Chapter Six apply here. . ."Go Easy" with the techniques that "Get Embarrassing."

There Are Four "GE" Techniques

The four "GE" Techniques involve reducing the wrong idea to·the absurd, laughing off an idea that has been overstated or extreme, questioning whether the other person really meant what he said and expressing his wrong idea or attitude in such a way as to force him to disagree with his earlier position.

GE-1   Reduces the wrong idea to the absurd.
GE-2   Involves "laughing off" an extreme position.
GE-3   Expresses doubt as to whether he really ment what he said.
GE-4   Involves agreeing with the wrong idea in such a way as to get him to disagree.

GE-1   Reduce The Wrong Idea To The Absurd

This, again, is the "reductio ad absurdum" often discussed in logic. Sometimes opposition to our ideas is based on a limitation or exception that will be ridiculous if made to apply generally. Moreover, it is quite common for some people to over-generalize. Think back to the case of the employment manager who thought all red-heads had bad tempers. Such a person may have had one or two bad experiences with a red-headed individual and he has permitted this limited experience to give him the privilege of making a generalization. When we encounter a situation in which our "opponent" in the face-to-face situation has over-generalized in this manner we have an opportunity to use GE-1.

The Sales Situation

A Purchasing Agent has said to a salesman, "You've got a stupid traffic department. I'm about to find a supplier that knows how to route shipments."

The salesman comes back, using a friendly smile as a preface, and says, "If you were right about that, our company would be bankrupt. Our sales and profits depend on getting our shipments completed in the best routing. Do you think Sears, Montgomery Ward and Allied would be buying from us if our traffic department were that bad? There's no question about the delay in this one shipment—but this is one in a thousand for our company."

Let's go back to the car prospect who said that his neighbor had said the car the salesman was selling was a "gas eater" because of the type of automatic transmission. If the salesman feels he can risk destroying the "neighbor," he might very well say: "Well, I don't know your neighbor, but if he feels that way he's probably the kind of a driver that floorboards the accelerator every time a light turns green. That's like a drag race! If a person is buying a car for drag racing, I sure wouldn't sell him an automatic transmission!"

The Supervisory Situation

Again we may go back to the man who doesn't want to wear his safety shoes. He says that there are times when his work is not dangerous and he ought to be able to wear regular shoes at those times. The supervisor says, "Yes, but I've seen the times when your work would shift back and forth to dangerous work several times in the day. If we let you change shoes every time your work was more or less hazardous, you'd be spending half your time walking between your work and your locker!"

A workman has complained to his supervisor because he has passed the number of days within which he is allowed to file a grievance. He feels he should be allowed to file his grievance, anyway. The supervisor says, "I suppose you think there shouldn't be any time limit on filing grievances. You feel we should just let them pile up until there were hundreds of them. The management and the union would have to take all their time for six months holding grievance sessions. Do you think that makes sense?"

A management trainee who takes issue with a major company policy might receive this kind of an answer from an executive: "That's a matter that has to be taken before the Executive Committee. I don't think they'd be willing to put you—a young man just a year out of college—on the agenda for one of their meetings."

The Family or Personal Situation

A father talks to his son who is protesting because he has to either be home by a certain hour or call to say where he is. "What do you want us to do when we wake up and find you're not in yet? Call the Missing Persons Bureau?"

Here's a husband whose wife has been over-spending on clothes: "Since I got this last promotion, it's true we're being invited out more. But at this rate, I'll be spending all of the raise I got to buy more clothes for you."

GE-2   "Laugh Off" An Extreme Statement Or Attitude

This particular technique has its principle value in situations in which another person has expressed an extreme position or made an over-statement in the "heat" of a discussion or argument. This happens at times. Under certain conditions, it becomes a valuable technique. You simply point out how extreme the position is to give the other person a chance to give it up and preserve his personal worth.

The Sales Situation

A salesman talking to a prospect about a living room suite is told by the prospect that another company has it for sale for $200 less. He replies: "You know, I'm going to get hold of the boss right away. This living room suite cost us more than that. I'm going to tell him he better start buying from North End Furniture if they're selling that cheap!"

A car prospect says that he can get the model he wants with all the features on one-week delivery from a competitor. The salesman says: "You know, if he had it in stock he could have showed it to you right then. And if he didn't have it in stock, it would take at least three weeks. It just can't be true. Let me tell you how cars like this have to be ordered."

The Supervisory Situation

Some skillful people use GE-2 by offering to make a bet that the claim can not be made good. For example, when a sales executive objected to a new compensation plan by saying, "All of our best man would quit," the chief executive came back: "You want to make a bet on that? I'll give you good odds. Actually, some of our best men will make more money under this arrangement."

A workman charges his supervisor with "wanting to break the union." The supervisor replies, "Man, I didn't know how important I was! Just think, here I am one supervisor out of over a hundred and you say that I'm trying to break the union. If I'm that important, I ought to be the plant superintendent."

The Family or Personal Situation

A young man who has received two moving traffic violations says the police officers have it "in for him." His father says, "You know, I think I had better talk to the Chief of Police about that. As short of policemen as we are, I don't think he can afford to have them trailing you around."

In the heat of a political discussion, a partisan says: "Why, that guy got rich from graft. I'll bet he picks up several thousand a year from kick-backs and that kind of stuff."

The reply: "Well, if you can prove it, you better go talk to the Internal Revenue Service. They'll give you a percentage of all the money they can collect, you know."

While GE-2 has its best value where it is used to combat an over-statement, it also has some usefulness where the "wrong" idea or attitude is comparatively unimportant. In such cases, the technique involves a wording which makes it ridiculous to waste time talking about it. "We've both got better things to do with our time than argue about that."

GE-3   Express Doubt That He Really Means What He Said

This is somewhat similar to GE-2. The difference lies in the possibility that this technique might result in a re-statement that is more acceptable or which might be opposed without starting an argument. The embarrassment comes from the implication that he could not really defend the position or the words he used.

The Sales Situation

The automobile salesman says, "Are you sure your wife objects to an automatic transmission? I was afraid I misunderstood you. Have you explained how an automatic transmission works—no clutch, no shifting?" The man finally admits that his wife was worried about the cost of the automatic transmission, not the way it operates.

When someone quotes a self-styled "safety" expert about automobile safety features, a salesman may use GE-3 in this way: "I know you were quoting (name of 'expert') on this safety feature, but do you really mean that he knows more about it than the engineers who have devoted their lives to studying such problems? Here's what their studies show."

The Supervisory Situation

A workman whose job has just been subject to a change in standards says that the Time Study men "have it in for him." The supervisor comes back: "Did I understand you correctly? You mean that they set this standard because they have a personal resentment of you? The man who worked on this standard has never done a time study job in our department before."

The sales executive is conferring with the accounting executive about a new report form that the accountant wants the salesmen to fill out. He says, "Look, Charlie, I filled out one of those daily report forms just as a test. It took me an hour to fill it out. If our boys make three calls in a day, that's going to take three hours additional time to fill in the report. Do you really mean that you expect our boys to do that?"

The Family or Personal Situation

A wife has said to her husband, "I'm never going to speak to that woman again!"

He comes back, "I wonder if you really mean that. After all, you're going to see her at PTA and at Church. It wouldn't be very Christian to hold a grudge like that. Besides, you don't know that she really said it. Maybe the person who told you exaggerated it."

A daughter has said, "If I have to be in by 12:30, the boys will quit asking me for dates."

Her mother replies, "That doesn't seem logical. Most of the girls have some time at which their parents expect them to be home. Do you really think you'll be a wallflower and get no bids to parties?"

GE-4 Agree With The "Wrong" Idea In Such A Way As To Get The Other Person To Disagree

As with the "D" techniques of presenting ideas, this technique works best with negativistic persons—those who always register disagreement. However, it is not solely applicable to such types. There are other situations in which a tentative type of agreement, skillfully phrased, can get the disagreement that you want. While the technique requires skill and sometimes forethought, it is very useful when the "right" occasion comes along.

Sometimes the technique may be prefaced by some phrase such as "O.K., just for the sake of argument, let's say you're right." At other times we might agree and say that it was for the purpose of clarification.

The Sales Situation

The car prospect has said that if he buys the Blastoff De Luxe they'll give him $200 more for his old car. Says the salesman: "All right, now let's suppose you make that deal just because they'll give you the $200 more for your present car. Then three years from now you'll have to trade in that Blastoff De Luxe. How do you think you'll come out?" The least that the prospect can say is that he doesn't know what will happen then. The salesman then clarifies the picture by showing comparisons of the trade-in values of Blastoff versus his car.

The prospect for an automatic washer has said to the salesman that he (and his wife) think it's only proper for them to "shop around" and look at competitive models. He tentatively agrees: "O.K. let's say you do shop around to look at the others. This is going to take quite a bit of time. You might prefer to take that time for a golf game." The customer sheepishly admits that he would rather play golf than "shop around." So the salesman says, "Well, if I were you, I'd rather play a game of golf, too. Over here we have a comparison chart showing all the features of all the brands. Let's go over it together and it may mean you can play golf instead of 'shopping around.' "

The Supervisory Situation

This supervisor is talking to a person who is negativistic and who is now protesting because the work standard requires him to get his own dies from the tool crib and get his own raw stock when he runs out. The supervisor says, "So, if you didn't have to get your own tools and materials, you'd save time. What would you do with that time?"

"I'd be able to make more parts and earn more bonus."

"And you think they wouldn't do a new time study under those conditions?"

"No, they always do a time study when changes like that are made (and he calls the time study department a dirty name)."

"Well, where do you think you'd wind up?"

"I suppose those dirty so-and-so's would make it even tougher to make bonus."

The supervisor clinches it: "Well, I don't think they're as bad as you say they are, but I think you're right. You might not come out as well off as you are now."

This chief executive has listened to an argument between the accounting executive and the sales executive about the controversial report form (see GE-3). He says to the accounting executive: "O.K., you say it takes only fifteen minutes and Joe says it takes an hour to fill out the report form you want. Now we're going to have a sales meeting, and if we adopt the report form, we'll have to show the boys how to use it. So you can give the boys a demonstration. You fill it out in fifteen minutes and Joe and I will go along with you." Obviously the Accounting Executive now has to "back down."

The Family or Personal Situation

This husband and wife are having a discussion about whether to buy the new car or the mink coat. He says, "O.K., suppose we buy the mink coat and forget about the new car. The tires on the old car have 25,000 miles on them. That's going to cost $150. The transmission is slipping, and that's another $100. If we keep it another year, my guess is we'll have $600 we'll have to spend above and beyond gas and oil. What will that do to our budget?" She has to agree that it will throw the budget out of kilter. Of course, he's only put off the evil day! She'll find a technique to convince him that the mink coat should come in a year or so.

The son wants a car to drive to school. "School" is 1,000 miles away. Father says, "O.K., so you get that new Bugaboo sport car. How much mileage does it get? How much does that amount to? How are you going to get that out of your allowance?" The answer is that it would cost too much to drive the car to and from "school." The son has to admit it.

To Get The Most Out Of This Chapter

Much as we would like to avoid such situations, there are times when we must "force" a wrong idea out of a person's mind by embarrassing him. So we have the "GE" techniques which "get embarrassing." But "GE" also has to stand for "go easy" because a person must be skillful in his use of these techniques. They are based on a loss of personal worth if the person does not give up the idea.

Take a piece of paper and write GE-1, GE-2, GE-3, and GE-4 on it. Now try to remember what each of the 4 techniques consists of. If you can't remember all of them, look them up.

Now write out an example of each, as you did in previous chapters. Take at least one example from each of three types of situations—sales, business, personal or family.

You should have twelve examples, three for each of the four techniques.

Now, for a final review of the ways to oppose or change "wrong" ideas or attitudes, put down the word "BRIDGE" to remind you that these techniques make a "bridge" between the "wrong" idea and your expression of opposition.

Then set the word up on your notepaper in vertical form:

B
R
I
D
G
E

Write down across from "BR" what it stands for. Do the same for "I" and for "D" and for "GE."

Special Note To Sales Supervisors

You can have one sales meeting in which you get your men to demonstrate each of the four GE techniques by role-playing. Have them create situations in which a customer or prospect has expressed an objection, then call on them to use a GE technique to oppose the objection. Have some discussion about the dangers involved. Where possible, show how a better technique might be substituted.

Have another sales meeting in which you "wrap up" all of the BRIDGE techniques and compare them for merit.

Chapter Eleven

HOW TO HANDLE "PROBLEM" PERSONALITIES

The person whose goal is to develop Power in dealing with people should not only develop skill in dealing with those who are typical individuals, but should also know how to handle those who are "different." Hence we include this chapter which discusses such special techniques as may be useful in handling "problem" personalities.

Defining The "Problem" Personality

The definition of a "problem" personality cannot begin with a phrase such as "What is a 'problem' personality?" or "Who is a 'problem' personality?" The truth is that all of us are "problem" personalities at some times for some of those around us. So our definition must be phrased, "*When* is a person a 'problem' personality?"

The important factor then, is timing. A person becomes a problem to us when his behavior is so unusual that ordinary methods are not successful in dealing with him.

The Factor Of Stress

We can say fairly confidently (in the light of modern research in the behavioral sciences) that a person becomes a "problem" when he is under unusual stress.

For our purposes we must define stress as "an excess of environmental pressure." All of us feel the pressure of problems presented to us by the environment in which we live. We must solve these problems in order to survive. We work at a job and this involves solving problems. We live with others who make demands on us—this, too, involves solving problems.

Whether it is the insurance premium that is due next month or concern about a son or daughter in college, our environment is continually demanding that we solve problems.

The most severe problem that a human being ever faces is fighting for survival on the battlefield. For this reason, military psychiatrists feel that a soldier should not be expected to remain "in continuous contact with the enemy" for too long a period of time. They feel that such stress will inevitably lead to mental illness if it lasts too long. In World War I they called it "shell-shock."

People Differ In Their Reaction To Stress

We cannot dismiss the discussion of stress, however, without bringing the element of individual differences into our definitions. Some individuals are very hardy and can tolerate more stress than others. Some are more sensitive to the demands that other people make of them, while others are more sensitive to the stress of frustration in reaching their goals. A type of stress that one person could tolerate might be very difficult for another person.

It is not just a matter of determining how much stress or how long the stress continues, but what kind of stress and what kind of stress-sensitivity is a part of the individual's makeup.

But Stress Is The Prime Ingredient

Despite all of these quantitative and qualitative sub-factors, the basic factor which causes a person to become a "problem" is stress—the pressure of unsolved environmental problems. Whether the end result is actual mental illness or just a temporary "problem" state for the individual, stress lies underneath as the causative factor.

Understanding, Not Criticism

Early in my studies in psychology, a very capable psychologist* gave me these words of warning: "If you are going to enter a career that involves psychology, you must learn to understand people, not criticize them; you must force yourself to explain why they behave as they do, not blame them for it."

This is essential. It is a prime pre-requisite for working with any type of "problem" personality.

When we criticize or blame a person we have lost our opportunity to get him to do what we want him to do. We have lost "contact" with him. So long as we "keep our cool" and work toward understanding him better, we are in communication with him. We have not isolated him, nor has he decided that we are just a part of his problem rather than a factor that contributes to the solution of his problem.

Understanding And Explaining Is Not "Excusing"

Some psychologists, psychiatrists, and social workers carry this idea so far that they seem to *excuse* "problem" behavior in others. I am not suggesting that you abandon your standards of behavior as you seek to understand another person. You are not excusing negative acts simply because you understand some of the reasons which account for such acts. Moreover, if you reflect understanding you may be able to help the other person to see the negative effects of his acts.

Search For The Stress That Underlies The "Problem"

The process of understanding involves a search for the sources of stress that are causative factors behind the

* Irvin T. Schultz, Ph.D.

"problem" state. Sometimes, as we will show later, this may become the key to effective handling of some "problem" personalities.

Two Types Of "Problem" Personalities

As a non-professional person, you will encounter two types of "problem" personalities: First, there are those that you are not able to change or influence under ordinary circumstances. These are persons who are actually in a state of mental illness or in a borderline state that is very close to it. Second, there are those who are under temporary stress or whose "problem" state is not so severe that you cannot deal with them by using special techniques.

You Are Not Qualified To "Cure" The Mentally Ill

The "problem" personality who is really ill "or close to it" cannot be handled effectively by the person who does not have professional training in psychiatry or clinical psychology. At best, we may be able to do some good by getting them to seek professional help. If we are unable to get them to seek professional help we can reflect an attitude of understanding which will not make them any worse. At worst, if we try to pressure them or do a bungling job of handling them, we may make them worse and they may harm themselves or others— maybe us!

How Do You Recognize The Mentally Ill Person?

Since you need to have some clues to the recognition of the person who is mentally ill, we should provide you with some knowledge about the way to recognize such persons.

In response to this need, two experts collaborated on a manual which helps the non-professional person recognize the signs of mental abnormality. Robert A. Matthews, M.D., and Loyd W. Rowland, Ph.D., sensing that this problem was one frequently faced by police officers, wrote a booklet "How To

Recognize And Handle Abnormal People—A Manual For The Police Officer." The manual was published by the National Association for Mental Helth during the period when I was an officer and director of that association. Dr. Rowland, a psychologist and a good friend of mine* had given me permission to reproduce the list of "telltale signs" shown on page 7 of this manual.

Nine "Telltale Signs" Of Mental Illness

These nine "telltale signs" are listed as follows:

"He shows big changes in behavior.
"He has strange losses of memory.
"He thinks people are plotting against him.
"He has grand ideas about himself.
"He talks to himself or hears voices.
"He sees visions, or smells strange odors, or has peculiar tastes.
"He thinks people are watching him or talking about him.
"He claims to have bodily ailments that are not possible.
"He behaves in a way that is dangerous to himself or others."

In subsequent pages Rowland and Matthews go more deeply into these "telltale" signs. If you desire additional knowledge about these signs, contact your local Chapter of the Mental Health Association for a copy of this manual. While especially slanted toward police officers, most of it is useful to the ordinary person who wants to learn more about recognizing the mentally ill.

The "Referral" Process

Since you are not trained in how to work with a person who exhibits the abnormalities described (above) the only help you can provide him is to try to get him to someone who can help him.

This process is called "referral" by those of us who are

---

* Dr. Rowland is now Director of Education and Research for the Louisiana Association for Mental Health.

familiar with the field of mental health and mental illness.

Sometimes, this referral may be direct referral to a mental health expert, at other times it may, of necessity, be indirect. If you have any doubts about your ability to make a direct referral, use the indirect method.

Definition Of "Direct" Referral

"Direct" referral is referring the person with abnormal behavior to a (1) Psychiatrist or (2) a Clinical Psychologist. A further definition is required for those of you who do not know the difference between these two types of specialists.

A *Psychiatrist* is a medical doctor who specializes in the diagnosis and treatment of the mentally ill. Do not make the mistake of judging psychiatry or psychiatrists on the basis of the jokes you have heard or read. The jokes, for the most part, refer to the psychiatrists who use a method called "psychoanalysis" (couch, long interviews, etc.). Most modern psychiatrists do not use psychoanalysis. They accomplish their diagnostic effort by using tests, modern drugs and other aids along with a thorough study of the individual's background. Obviously, a psychiatrist is essential if the abnormal person must be hospitalized, since psychologists are not admitted to general hospital staffs. However, most psychiatrists have an association with a clinical psychologist to make the maximum use of the special talents of their profession.

A *Clinical Psychologist* is a person with graduate training in *psychotherapy.* This is the process of re-training a person's thinking habits back to a more "normal" state. Most clinical psychologists have a Ph.D. degree and a period of special internship in their field. They are experts in diagnostic tests, too, as a result of their extensive academic training.

Both of these specialists are listed in the yellow pages of your telephone book. Psychiatrists are listed under the medical specialties on the pages headed "Physicians and Surgeons" under the sub-heading: "Nervous and Mental Diseases (Psychiatry)." Psychologists are listed under "Psychologists" and in some directories they are identified as "Clinical Psychologists" after the listing of their names.

174 HOW TO HANDLE "PROBLEM" PERSONALITIES

Making A "Direct" Referral

Individuals whose behavior is clearly abnormal tend to resist direct referrals. They have probably lost insight and feel that "everyone else is out of step." They may feel that they are normal and everyone else is abnormal.

If you say: "You should see Dr. Blank," you are likely to get the reply: "So you think I'm nuts, huh?" or "Why should I go to a head-shrinker? There's nothing wrong with me." If you make this mistake, your only way out is to defend your position by saying: "No, I don't think you're nuts, but I think you should talk to someone who knows more about your problem and the way to solve it than I do. Dr. Blank is an expert. He deals with this kind of problem all the time."

It is better to use some adaptation of the techniques described in Chapters Four, Five and Six and present your referral idea in such a way that it has a better chance of acceptance. "One of my friends went to Dr. Blank to talk over a problem like yours. . ." or "You will remember that modern psychiatrists (psychologists) run into all sorts of problems and you can talk to them in complete confidence." If it happens to be a person who has had a "big change" in his behavior, you could say: "I've known you for quite awhile and I've noticed lately that you're not the same person you used to be. Maybe this change is good for you, but in order to be sure you ought to take the time to talk to an expert like Dr. Blank."

Obviously, a direct referral is usually limited to a situation in which (a) You know the person well, (b) He is a subordinate to you in the work situation, or (c) He has asked you for advice or told you his troubles.

Making An "Indirect" Referral

For most people the most practical way to make a referral is indirectly—through an intermediary.

The abnormal person is less likely to resent or refuse this type of referral. He can't say "Oh, you think I'm nuts," or start telling stories about "head-shrinkers."

Referrals of this type may be made to *anyone who knows more about mental illness and psychology than you do!*

A list of such persons could become a very long list, too long for this book. We'll just put down 12 such types of persons who can serve as indirect referrals. Most of them will have more skill in making a direct referral than you do. Also, they will have contacts which make it easier for them to set up an appointment with a psychiatrist or a clinical psychologist.

Medical Doctors—Physicians
Lawyers
Police Officers
Juvenile Officers
Ministers
School and College Counselors
School and College Psychologists
Industrial Psychologists
Social Workers
Personnel Counselors
Mental Health Association Chapters
Community Mental Health Centers.

Which of these "intermediaries" you select for an indirect referral depends on the individual. For parents, for example, the school counselors are the most convenient intermediaries. In business situations, industrial psychologists and personnel counselors are most convenient. For church-goers, the minister is often the best referral, especially if he has had training in recognizing and handling the mentally ill.

If you desire advice concerning a referral, you can get good counsel from the local chapter of the Mental Health Association or from a Community Mental Health Center. In this way you can receive more specific guidance than we can provide here.

So much for your handling of the individual who exhibits the signs of mental illness. Now let's discuss the other type—the person who is a "problem," but does not show the telltale signs described earlier.

Stress Is Still The Important Factor For These Types, Too

As we indicated earlier, the stress which a person feels is a prime contributing factor to the "problem" personality. For the mentally ill, the stress has become intolerable and this has driven them to their abnormal state. The same is true of the lesser types of "problem" personality. Stress lies at the bottom of their "problem" state, but it has not caused them to reach the abnormal level.

Again: Understanding, Not Criticism

The more you know about the "problem" personality, the better able you are to cope with his problem state and keep him effective. You will have more power to deal with him if you understand him. If you blame or criticize him you will lose your chance to change him.

This is especially true with respect to the stress such an individual faces. If you can find out the nature of his unsolved problems you may be able to help him solve them, but, at the very least, you will understand him better.

EIGHT TYPES OF "BORDERLINE" CASES

In my extensive experience in testing and counseling management and supervisory persons, I have found that the eight types of personality described by the Minnesota Multiphasic Personality Inventory fit certain patterns of "problem" personalities. They are not so extreme as to be "abnormal," but they provide problems for those who must deal with them. Instead of using technical language, I'll use the language commonly employed by their associates to describe their behavior.

1. The person who imagines that he is "sick."
2. The discouraged person who "gives up" easily.
3. The tense, anxious person.
4. The undisciplined person who is not "on the team."
5. The over-defensive person.
6. The alarmist.
7. The day-dreamer.
8. The wheel-spinning eager-beaver.

Each of these types, with additional stress, may become

abnormal and call for referral. So long as they do not show the behavior described by the nine "telltale" signs, you may be able to handle them with some effectiveness.

1. The Person Who Imagines He Is "Sick"

While not a real hypochondriac, this type of person uses his body as an excuse for poor performance. This type of person commonly contributes materially to absenteeism in the work situation. Listening to his recitals of false symptoms and exaggerated petty illness will cause him to like you, but may prove expensive in terms of your time and his—"company" time. If you can put up with it at coffee breaks, lunch, etc., he'll think you're a "nice guy." Perhaps the best solution is to recommend a doctor to him or ask him when he last had a complete and thorough physical examination.

But remember: He is facing some stress that he has not resolved. He is blaming his physical condition for his inability to achieve. If you can show him that he is actually making progress on the job (in school, in his hobby) and if you can help him solve the problems he faces, you will make him more effective.

2. The Discouraged Person

Dr. Rowland did not mention the extremely-depressed person in his list of nine "telltale" signs. However, later in the same manual he devotes a chapter to it. I would recommend that chapter to you. Actually, Dr. Rowland had the extremely-depressed person in mind in describing the person "dangerous to himself." These are potential suicides and must be referred to professionals—quickly.

However, a person who has suffered the loss of a loved one or who has had several set-backs in his progress may simply show discouragement and a sort of lassitude—a "slowing down." He "gives up" on a problem that he should be able to solve.

Three types of activity on your part may help you to handle this person effectively:

    a. If he works for you, get him to agree to a schedule of

activity that is close to his normal output. Then follow-up periodically, using good tact and technique, to keep him aware of his commitment. In my experience, the stimulus of added activity as presented by a supervisor, tends to pull the person out of his discouragement. Sales managers help such a person by giving him an easy prospect to close.

b. Recognize the fact that he is "down in the dumps." Tell him so, with an understanding expression and a hand on his shoulder. If you know why he is "down," let him know that you know (provided it can be done in good taste).

c. Encourage him. Compliment him for good work and actual achievement.

3. The Tense, Anxious Person

This is the over-controlled type of person, very cautious about face-to-face situations (sometimes to the degree that he puts off "people" problems). He may suffer from some mild physical disorders that are caused by his tension and anxiety—but that's a matter for him and his physician!

You can work effectively with this type of person if you help him develop maturity in facing the unusual and difficult problem that upsets the routine (See Chapter 15—"Maturity In Facing The Unexpected"). If you present your idea as a challenge to him, you will have a better chance to get his acceptance of it. Since he has a tendency to put off or procrastinate about problems involving people, encourage him to get these problems out of the way first.

If you are in a position to do so, encourage this person to get physical recreation and relaxation.

4. The Undisciplined Person

The person who is basically not "on the team" and not willing to accept the disciplines that are necessary to group living is very hard to handle. He is quite likely to say "yes" to what you want him to do and then do nothing about it—a pretty difficult problem for a supervisor. While he does not think that he is "lying," he definitely shades the truth in his own favor. He may appear to contradict himself as a result of this tendency—he says what suits the occasion and if the occasion justifies it (in his opinion) he may take a position that is opposite to a previous one.

Three special techniques are required in dealing with these undisciplined types:

a. Take advantage of opportunities to teach him the fundamental facts of group or social living: We derive advantage from being a part of a group, team, community, organization. The rules made by such groups are designed to preserve the group's very existence (laws, ethics, codes, mutual cooperation and teamwork). Behavior that departs from these established limits and disciplines hurts the group and threatens its survival.

b. If this person is a subordinate whom you must train, increase the thoroughness of your follow-up and be sure that the "right" way has become a conditioned habit.

c. At a time when such a person engages in undisciplined behavior, immoral, unethical, or illegal acts, you must make it clear to him that the ultimate results of such acts will be ostracism from the social group. Show him what happens to those who persist in such behavior. This involves the "forcing techniques" of Chapters Six and Ten.

If you find that this person has done something "behind your back" or has been guilty of "talking out of both sides of his mouth," confront him with the evidence promptly.

5. The Over-Defensive Person

This is the individual who always thinks of the reasons why some idea won't work. If a new procedure is proposed, he finds reasons why no change should be made. This rigidity and defensiveness stems from rather deep-seated feelings. He feels he should have thought of the new idea first. He feels that his personal worth is being challenged by anything in the nature of change.

If you present ideas to him with a sincere effort to build his personal worth, if you concentrate on making him feel that he has a part in the plans, you will find him easier to work with.

As indicated in a previous example, if you can make him feel that he is the only one who can make your idea work (because of special abilities and/or experience) he may give you that extra motivation that will make your idea a great success.

6. The Alarmist

You will encounter "problem" people who always "make a mountain out of a molehill." Usually you will find that the "mountain" gives them an excuse to avoid working on a more difficult problem that really has a higher priority. While the higher priority can be established by discussion and reasoning, this person will still provide a problem in his ongoing work and attitudes. He will tend to miss deadlines, suffer from poor concentration (with possible error as a result) and become sidetracked by petty problems.

As a result, so long as this person is in this "problem" state you must follow-up frequently. You must check his schedule and his priorities regularly. Encourage him to make a list of his problems, duties, projects and put a priority number in front of each. He should then follow this order of priority in his daily (or hourly or weekly) work.

There are times when the alarmist may be "kidded" out of his over-concern. "Look, man, we've got a lot of things that are more important right now."

7. The Day-Dreamer

In working with the person who is inclined to day-dream and get separated from the practical, real world, we should keep him in touch with reality by the same methods used for the alarmist. His good ideas may have some value for the future, but his assignments must be completed in a proper order of priority.

As you talk to this type of person, visual aids (pad, pencil, etc.) will help to hold his attention.

Try to help him adapt his creative thinking to the work-a-day practical world. "That's a good idea. Let's see how we could actually put it into practice. Set up a timetable and bring me a sequence of things that would accomplish that end."

When you have completed instructions for a person of this type, ask him to tell you what you told him. Listen carefully to be sure he has not left out some important step.

8. The Wheel-Spinning Eager Beaver

This is the person (Chapter 15) who has a powerful engine and pushes the accelerator but who doesn't use the brake!

It is important, here, to point out that there are situations in which an otherwise eager and well-motivated person goes through "wheel-spinning" periods or phases. For example, young men just graduating from college or just out of the military service have this tendency. Also, young women who are to be married in sixty to ninety days tend to go through this phase.

A supervisor needs to accentuate his follow-up effort for a person in this "problem" phase. He should also emphasize the importance of checking new ideas or activities before going ahead with them.

Any person who deals with someone in this mood or phase needs to emphasize caution and warn him against impetuous activity or activity that is not purposeful.

While this person is readily angered, he gets over it quickly. You can be very frank with him (or her).

Since many executives go through phases of this type, it is well to remember that the stalling and slowing-down techniques should be used with them (Chapter Nine—Delaying Techniques).

Search For The Source Of Stress

Just as the mentally ill have succumbed to stress that was intolerable to them, so the lesser types of "problem" personalities reach their state because of stress that exceeds the "normal" amount for them. (There is an exception for both types—the situation in which there is a bodily disorder or illness. This can only be discovered by a thorough physical examination.)

Sometimes the source of stress is obvious. The extremely discouraged person whose wife or child is ill is an example. Also the young woman about to be married is a similar example. She "spins her wheels" because she has difficulty keeping her mind on her work!

Fortunately, in many supervisory and administrative situations, the source of stress is, at times, obvious. In talking to a group of Certified Public Accountants, I said: "From March 1 to April 15 (income-tax time!) you're going to run into more problem people than any other time of the year. Every accountant in your office is working overtime and frantically trying to meet the deadline. It's natural that he should be more of a problem at this time. Just take it for granted. Expect it. When you run into snags in dealing with your fellow C.P.A.'s, laugh it off: 'We're suffering from an occupational disease that occurs every year at this time.' "

Watch For Seasonal Peaks

This same source of stress is inevitable in businesses with seasonal peaks. I make it a rule to work very cautiously with clients who are automobile dealers during the period in which they are preparing for the introduction of new models. They have a lot of problems to solve at that time!

Again: Understanding Is Important

If you know that a person is facing extra stress or problems, the fact that you show understanding makes him easier to deal with. Expressions of that understanding help even more. If, as a supervisor, you can help a subordinate reduce his stress by showing him easier ways to get over the difficult period, you will find him grateful and his gratitude will take the form of increased motivation.

To Get The Most Out Of This Chapter

Put down the names of at least three persons with whom you work or whom you know personally.

After each name make a notation of a time when that person was under unusual stress. Then put a number after his (or her) name that matches one of the 8 types of "problem" personalities which we described in this chapter. Think of ways in which you might have handled them more effectively.

Go to the local office of your Mental Health Association and ask them to loan you a copy of the pamphlet "How To Recognize And Handle Abnormal People." They may not have the manual for police officers, but will have a substitute or tell you where you can find one.

Look in the yellow pages of your telephone directory to find "Psychiatrists" and "Psychologists." You may need to refer to this at some time in the future when an emergency occurs!

Go back to the list of persons (this chapter) to use as indirect referral aides. Check that list to see how many such persons you know.

Chapter Twelve

THE TIME
AND THE PLACE TO
"GET TOUGH"

This chapter may seem to be out of place in this book. All of the material we have presented to this point, emphasizes the avoidance of threats, the soft-pedalling of forcing techniques and satisfying the basic needs for personal worth and security in those with whom you work. I have stressed the idea that you should get people to do what *you* want them to do because *they* want to do it.

With the exception of some examples involving techniques that have elements of forcing the other person to accept ideas or lose personal worth or to give up wrong attitudes for the same reason (Chapters Six & Ten), we have implied that the person who develops Power in dealing with people never "gets tough" with others.

That is true, generally speaking. But there are times when people who have developed Power in dealing with others find it necessary and desirable to use methods which are not in keeping with the general tenor of this book.

The Exception That Proves The Rule

As I study those who have great power in dealing with people I find that all of them use stronger methods at times. They "get tough" occasionally. And while the times and the places at which they use strong methods are few and far between, these exceptions must be taken into account if you are to round out your power to deal with people. To use an old saw: "This is the exception that proves the rule." As you will see in this chapter, these situations are really exceptions. They are not the day-in-day-out relationships with which we have been dealing to this point in this book.

A List Of Conditions Under Which "Getting Tough" Is Called For

You will have to consider carefully when there is a time and place that call for using "get tough" methods. However, a brief list of some of the situations that call for such methods may be helpful. Here's such a list:

1. To prevent someone from imposing on you.
2. To get action when time is a factor.
3. To avoid danger and in emergencies.
4. To get attention instead of a "brush-off."
5. To prevent involvement in an unethical or illegal act.

Preferably, these conditions should be accompanied by other factors such as:

a. You have nothing important to lose by "getting tough."
b. You will never have to deal with this person again.
c. There is no need for continuing motivation on the part of the other person after your immediate goal is accomplished.
d. The person is clearly an "abnormal" person of a certain type that requires strong stimuli.

Let's study these factors and conditions a little more closely and consider examples.

To Prevent Imposition

You will encounter situations in which people will attempt to impose on you. Sometimes you will find the techniques of Chapters Seven, Eight, Nine and Ten very useful. If the effort to impose on you persists beyond reason, you must "get tough."

There are obvious examples, as when someone attempts to steal a place in a waiting line at a ticket window. To preserve your personal integrity and build your strong personality you must object to such behavior. It is not necessary to start a fight—all you need to do is to call out: "The end of the line is back there!" Then point to the end of the line. You must raise your voice, of course, if the person is a distance from you. Also, raising your voice serves the purpose of getting the attention of the others in the line (who are also being imposed upon). Raising your voice will also make it possible to enlist the cooperation of others in the line if the place-stealer becomes belligerent. However, I would point out that such a person almost always recognizes he is in the wrong and knows that the whole group will be against him if he causes trouble.

Sometimes when you are very busy another person may try to waste your time by talking about Sunday's golf or pro football game. You will just have to say: "Look—I'm working against a four o'clock deadline and I just can't take time out." Admittedly, this is not very "tough," but it is a little less courteous than most of the methods we have emphasized.

To Get Action When Time Is A Factor

Occasionally you will encounter people who should give you prompt and efficient service, but who are under-motivated (or, perhaps, over-worked). They must be jarred, literally, into giving you the service to which you are entitled.

The Case Of The "Loused Baggage"

An example stands out vividly in my mind. We had a young woman executive who arrived on a mid-afternoon plane. Her baggage was not on the plane. It was lost. After they had determined that the baggage had not come off the plane (or had never been on it since her last transfer point) she talked to the man in charge of lost baggage, describing it, filling out forms. I stood in the background, listening.

"When you find it, how soon will it get here?"

"Well, I can't say, lady. We'll do our best. Surely it will be here by morning. Maybe before midnight. They'll put it on the first plane coming here after they find it.

Almost in tears, she said, "But there's a party tonight and my dress and all of my cosmetics are in my bags."

"Well, like I say, lady, we'll do our best." He was quite obviously not showing the motivation that she deserved under the circumstances.

I stepped up to the desk alongside her. "I've got news for you," I said. "She needs her dress and cosmetics for an 8 o'clock dinner party. You have two planes—one from each direction—that will arrive here in time for her to get to the party. She might be a little late if they carried the bag on from here, but if they missed it when she transferred it will be easy to bring it in on the plane that gets here at 6:30. All you have to do is get on that telephone."

"Well, we use the ticker for things like this and it's not that fast."

"You haven't heard the rest of the news I've got for you. If her bag doesn't get in on one of those two planes, your airline is going to buy her a new dress, new underclothing, new cosmetics, a new wardrobe. The shops are open tonight and she'll have time to get them if you don't get her stuff here."

"Yessir, well maybe I better call right now." He picked up the phone and started to work. The bags arrived on the next plane from her transfer point where they had been left!

We got action by "getting tough."

The Case Of The "Clip" Joint

In a major city, a group of fellows went to a bar-and-burlesque spot. It was not too reputable and they should not have gone, of course. They sat down close to the strip show and even bought the girls some drinks between their acts. When they got their bill it was just over $200 and for at least four times as many drinks as they ordered, including the ones for the girls. The fellow who had the check called for the manager. The manager refused to make any change in the check. "That's what you got. That's what you'll pay for." The argument dragged on. They had called a cab and it was waiting.

Finally, one of the biggest fellows in the crowd stood up (six feet four and 210 pounds). "I'll take that check. You guys go call a cop and take the cab. I'll wait here."

The manager changed his tune immediately. He called the waiter. "Must have been a mistake here." The bill was settled for a fraction because the "big" man "got tough" and he got action. He prevented an imposition as well.

"Get Tough" In Emergencies Or To Avoid Danger

When there is imminent danger or an emergency exists, you will find it necessary to raise your voice or even take physical action. This is probably the reason that military officers are selected partly on the basis of a strong and commanding voice. They may need that strong voice to be heard above the sounds of battle!

If your voice is not powerful, you can do things to make it more powerful. Try to keep the pitch toward the low range if you have a high-pitched voice. Enunciate clearly (see Chapter Fourteen).

Examples of the need for "getting tough" in an emergency are many. If a person is severely injured in an accident, your First Aid tells you that he should not be moved until the nature of his injuries has been determined by an expert. If someone starts to move him you must cry, "Stop! Don't move him. You may kill him." If a person is about to do something dangerous (such as touching an electric appliance when he is soaking wet around a swimming pool) you may have to push him away or cry out to stop him.

On a hunting trip, one of my friends who is very strongly committed to safety saw a member of our hunting group start to crawl through a barbed-wire fence with his gun not on "safety." "Stop, Charley!" Charley stopped. "Put your gun on safety before you ever crawl through a fence. A lot of guys have gotten killed that way."

The Case Of The Suicidal Driver

An executive told me of a time when he "got tough" with one of his associates, actually his boss. They were driving home on a high speed road. The man had been pouring out his troubles. His wife had "caught him in the act" and was divorcing him. He had just learned this in a long distance call from his lawyer. He was also worried about his son who wasn't doing very well in college. Also, he had a hangover from heavy drinking at a meeting the night before.

As he continued to pour out his troubles, he mentioned his heavy accident insurance coverage and, as they passed an over-pass abutment, he said something to the effect that "If you'd hit one of those things it would finish you off quick."

The junior executive took charge. He reached over and turned off the engine switch, held the wheel while the car slowed down. He took the key out of the ignition, opened the door, and said: "I'm driving." As he got around to the driver's side he added: "Get in the back seat."

"Why?"

"Because I don't want you anywhere near the wheel of the car."

"Getting tough" may have saved two lives. The man who had threatened suicide was later hospitalized for depression.

How To Get Attention Instead Of A "Brush-off"

The "get tough" methods may be useful at times to gain the attention of someone who otherwise might give you the "brush-off."

In many cases the words you use may not be "tough" words, but they are words which describe expensive or dangerous consequences and as a result force attention. Sometimes they are words or phrases which imply that you feel you are being "brushed off."

Let's take a few examples:

"Apparently you don't think this is very important. Let me point out. . ."

A union leader was giving the "brush-off" to an industrial relations man who was protesting the violence of pickets. "You're making a mountain out of a molehill."

"Maybe I am," he replied, "but our general counsel says that we can sue both you and the union if company property is damaged. Keep that in mind."

A subordinate slowed down a chief executive who was about to take impulsive action by saying, "Before you do that, call up our general counsel and see what he says." This got the desired effect. The chief executive dropped the idea.

If another person takes a threatening posture and refuses your efforts to calm him down, you may get his attention by implying that the conversation is reaching the stage at which a lawsuit might result. "We will have to start talking through our lawyers. We're not getting anywhere. Anything we might say now might have to be repeated in court."

The Case Of The "Manic" Executive

An executive was referred to me by the head of a company because he had alienated all of his subordinates. In the referral, his boss had told him that he would either have to "shape up or ship out" because things had reached an intolerable point. Important subordinates were threatening to leave the company. Morale in his division of the company was at rock-bottom levels.

When he told his boss that he "didn't know what he was doing wrong" and asked, "What am I supposed to do?", his boss simply said, "I'm not an expert in matters like these. Why don't you go over and see Bentley Barnabas. Maybe he'll give you some tests that will find out what's the matter."

When the tests were in, I realized that the man was probably in a state which we call "manic" and that it appeared to have reached abnormal levels. When he came over to talk to me about the results, the following conversation took place.

"Well, what about those damned tests I took?"

"Charley, the tests tell me that you should see Dr. Jones (a psychiatrist that he knew)."

"You mean you want me to see a head-shrinker?"

"Exactly."

"The heck with that. He'd try to change me. I'm satisfied with me the way I am. Now what about those tests?"

"I'm sorry. I can't discuss them with you. If you want to talk about the weather or golf, O.K. But I can't talk to you about you."

"Why?"

"Well, you just confirmed what the tests say. You have no insight. You seem to be incapable of self-criticism. You're right and everyone else is wrong. That means that you are beyond the reach of an industrial psychologist. You need a clinical psychologist or a psychiatrist."

"You're saying that I'm nuts. What have you got to prove it?"

"I said we wouldn't talk about you anymore."

For three days he tried to get me to "talk" with him. Each time I refused to do it. Bluntly, too.

On the fourth day he asked me to make an appointment with Dr. Jones. He was successfully treated and now heads a large company.

You May "Get Tough" To Avoid An Unethical Or Illegal Act

As a person reaches positions of leadership or authority he may at times be approached by those who would make it seem desirable to commit an act which is either illegal or unethical (or at least "borderline"). In such cases you have to "get tough" to jar the other person into a realization of the possible consequences to you, to him, or to both of you.

For example, when a union leader subtly implied that a "pay-off" to him might solve certain problems for a company, the chief executive made it clear that the government could take action against both the union and the company if the act were discovered. The union leader dropped the subject and was much less troublesome thereafter.

"I Won't Commit Perjury"

A utility executive told me how he handled a prominent politician who solicited a campaign contribution. The politician actually knew the act was illegal (The Public Utility Act of 1935 forbade utility companies contributing to political campaigns) because he asked that the contribution be made in postage stamps—$500 worth!

The utility executive "got tough" in a subtle way. He said: "I'll take this up with the boss, because he would have to O.K. any expenditure of this type. However, even if he approves, I want to make one thing clear: I will not commit perjury under any circumstances and if I am asked about this I will have to tell the whole truth." The politician did not come back!

Blackmail—Expressed Or Implied

In my experience I have talked to several individuals who have been approached by persons who either expressed or implied blackmail—"If you don't do this, I'll expose you." Blackmail is a criminal act. In each of the cases, the individual foiled the blackmailer by the simple process of saying: "That's blackmail. It's against the law. Do your worst."

One prominent person told me a rather unique way in which he "got tough" with a blackmailer. "Have you got a plane reservation to get out of town?" he asked. The would-be blackmailer said: "No, why do you ask?" "Because if I were to pay you off, the next thing I would do would be to call the District Attorney and charge you with blackmail. If you were still in town you'd find yourself under indictment." The blackmailer backed down.

A Quote From Theodore Roosevelt

President Theodore "Teddy" Roosevelt made a statement which applies to all situations in which you may decide to "get tough" for the reasons we have outlined in this chapter. He said: "If you decide to hit a man, hit him with all your might. If you don't intend to hit him with all your might, don't hit him at all."

If you reach a person-to-person situation in which circumstances justify a "get tough" position, don't "pull your punches." If you feel that "getting tough" involves too much risk, use the techniques we described in earlier chapters.

To Get The Most Out Of This Chapter

Brush up on your use of imperatives—commands. Think of words and phrases that are arresting, attention-getting.

See if you can think of a situation in which each of the following might have justified a "get tough" approach:

1. Someone was imposing on you, or trying to.
2. You needed to get action when time was a factor.
3. There was impending danger or an emergency.
4. You needed to get attention from someone who was giving you a "brush off."
5. Someone was attempting to get you to do something "borderline"—either ethically or legally.

Chapter Thirteen

HOW TO
GET PEOPLE TO
REMEMBER YOU

Developing your power to deal with people involves another important aspect: You want to get them to remember you. While this is especially important if your success depends upon "repeat" contacts with the same individuals, it has its value in any contact that you make.

Some people have a natural talent for this and it contributes to their success. Sometimes it involves "charm," sometimes just distinctive speech, dress or appearance in general.

How much of this is natural and inborn is hard to say. Nevertheless, in studying people who enjoy great success in dealing with others, one outstanding observation is this: People remembered them. With or without charm they were remembered and this contributed to their power in dealing with people.

Remember: You Are The Stimulus

It will not be your ideas that constitute the prime stimulus to power in dealing with people. It will be YOU. In our study of the stimulus-response conditioning that changes human behavior we emphasized that the Stimulus is YOU. We pointed out that the product a salesman sells may be seen and appreciated only in the representation he makes of it to the prospect or customer. HE becomes a part of the Product. Cold, and without the presentations which bring the product warmth and utility, some products would not sell. The product could not sell itself (except in very rare cases).

We also emphasized that the response of the other person is action that is favorable to your cause, your success. For the purposes of this chapter, the response is getting them to remember who you are, what you stand for, what you want them to do.

Review: The Ways To Strengthen Your Stimulus

In Chapter Two we set out five ways to strengthen a stimulus. Let's review them briefly:

1. Create a stimulus which strikes the sense organ with greater impact (louder to the ears, larger to the eyes, etc.).
2. Present the stimulus in such a way that it gets greater receptivity (techniques).
3. Present the stimulus to two or more sense organs at the same time.
4. Evoke images or recollections which get secondary stimulation from other brain areas.
5. Tie our stimulus to the previous conditioning of the other person.

These are all very useful in getting others to remember you and to remember you favorably.

The stronger your stimulus as a personality, the more certain they are to remember you.

Make The Opening Stimulus Strong!

When you meet a person, even if you have been introduced by someone else, make it a point to repeat your name clearly. Don't mumble it, don't let your voice trail off, say it so that even a person with some hearing loss can't miss it!

If you meet a man and shake hands do it with some strength (but don't hurt him). Grip his hand firmly. One man that I know and remember always turns his right wrist to the left as he shakes hands, turning your hand with it. Since his name is Steel, this strong hand shake and turning action has created an image in my mind.

Use Your First Name With Your Surname

Don't be Mister Smith! Be Jim Smith or Joe Smith or Clem Johnson. While there are exceptions, of course, most successful people use their first names. To get the best remembrance out of your name, drop the middle initial unless it is necessary to identify you. If another person starts out to "Mister" you, use some unusual device to get him to use your first name. My method is quite simple. When someone calls me "Mister Barnabas," I quickly say, "Mister Barnabas was a fine old gentleman, but he died several years ago. I'm his son, Bentley."

Get A Nickname And Use It

Dwight David Eisenhower became "Ike" early in life and it helped him to become President of the United States. Remember "I Like Ike"—the slogans and buttons of the 1952 campaign?

If someone comes up with an interesting nickname for you, latch onto it and use it. For personal correspondence sign your name with your nickname. Always, nickname or not, sign your letters "Joseph James," not "J. H. James."

If there is a common nickname that you don't like, make it

clear in a positive way. I know a girl who always says "Elizabeth Jones—but it's Betty and not Liz." This helps her to be remembered, but also gets away from the "Liz" that she doesn't like.

When she was a little girl someone gave Mrs. A. Felix DuPont the nickname of "Marka" for her real name of "Martha." Everyone knows her by her nickname and it adds to the great charm and warmth which characterizes her as a great lady.

Don't accept a nickname that is a diminutive. Don't be a "Buster," a "Billy," a "Shorty," or a "Sissy" (for a girl). Simply substitute your preferred nickname. "My name is the same as my father's, but I prefer 'Bill' to 'Junior.' " "When I was in grade school they called me 'Buster,' but now I'm 'Chuck.' "

Bring Something Into Your Introduction That Helps Them To Remember You

Regardless of your name, you can bring something to your introduction which helps to give your identity. I know a man named Jones who carefully says "Spelled J-O-N-E-S." This not only gets a laugh, but it gets a lot of people to remember him. Another: "Johnston—spelled with a 'T.' " Others: "Smyth spelled with a 'Y,' " "Knott spelled with a 'K,' " "Brewer—as in a beer factory." When I meet a person I sometimes say "Barnabas—spelled the same as St. Barnabas in the Bible. But that's where the resemblance ends!"

Another example of a trick memory device was one invented by Rolle R. Rand, a Chamber of Commerce Executive and writer. His personal correspondence was signed R^3. If it weren't such an obvious theft of an original idea, I'd steal it and sign my name B^2!

A man named Smith was from the town of Smith Center. He always says: "Sam Smith from Smith Center—but they didn't name the town after me." People not only remember his name, but his home town!

Get Originality Into Your Vocabulary

One sure way to help people to remember you is to get original phrases and words into your ordinary speech. Avoid cliches unless you make apologies for them, but make the apology itself have some interest. If you quote an old saw like "haste makes waste" add the phrase "As my grandmother always said." Or add: "To coin a phrase."

The use of appropriate figures of speech to brighten your conversation will be discussed in the chapter "Be Sure They Are Reading You 'Loud and Clear.' " That chapter is devoted to strengthening the presentation of an idea. Here we are talking about devices to help people to remember you. While there is an inter-relation between the two chapters, this one has to do with individuality and the associated originality.

Examples Of Interesting Words And Phrases

In my acquaintance I find some interesting examples of originality in words and phrases that help people remember the person who was there. One friend of mine coined a phrase to indicate an undercut in Gin Rummy. If he undercuts you he says: "I caught a man speeding." If it is a "deep" undercut he adds "And in a school zone, too!"

A man who attended the Harvard school for executives replaced the phrase "I don't know" with "They didn't teach that at Harvard."

The word "gismo" came into the vocabulary about twenty years ago, but one man always describes some intricate mechanical device as a "gismoid." For him a difficult mechanical task is a "tool job."

A friend who is in the steel-jobbing business always answers the question: "How's the steel business?" with "You want to buy some?"

One executive, a former athlete, admits a mistake by saying: "I'd sure like to play that one over."

All such devices will help you to get people to remember you.

Present Your Stimulus To More Than One Sense Organ

To employ a stronger stimulus to get people to remember you, use one that strikes more than one sense organ in the other person. Obviously, the sense of taste cannot be involved. Women can use a distinctive scent to help get their individuality ⸮cross—although they should be careful not to use too much! The prime sense organs for getting people to remember you are the eyes, the ears, and the sense of touch. Naturally, the latter is the one that is least used by most of us.

As you meet a person and converse with him, the prime receptor is the sense of sound. Don't overlook the fact of a distinctive appearance, however. That will be discussed later.

The handshake should be firm, not too much pressure. This adds a distinctive stimulus to the sense of touch, but it is not the only one that will help you to be remembered. I remember one man because he frequently puts his left hand on my shoulder as he is shaking hands. This adds warmth, friendliness to his greeting. Another comes up and pats me on the back. Another puts his left hand on my wrist as he shakes hands with the right, gripping it just lightly. Still another puts his left hand on top of the handshake.

I would strongly recommend to women that they offer their hand when they meet a man. While it is not considered proper for a man to offer his hand, it is a gesture of warmth and interest for a woman to offer hers. A man should never grip a woman's hand in the way he would a man's hand—just hold it briefly with very slight pressure.

Appearance As A Factor In Getting People To
Remember You

A distinctive appearance will help people to remember you and thus increase your power with people. Women have the advantage over men in this area, since their clothing is more colorful and distinctive. Men are getting more opportunity to do the same thing in current styles, however.

For men, distinctive cufflinks, initials on shirts, distinctive pocket handkerchiefs and ties are helpful. Get a "pattern" of distinctiveness about your clothing (within the limits of changing fashion) and stick with it. This will help people to remember you.

Because my wife likes blue colors, my neckties, handkerchiefs, and sportscoats emphasize blue. My friends have noticed this and comment on it. I explain that my wife likes blue, "And since I don't spend my time looking at myself, it makes little difference to me. She has to look at me a lot!"

Several of my friends have made a hobby of distinctive cuff links. Others have unusual initials on their shirt pockets. Years ago I had my initial "B" put on the cuffs of my shirts. This, too, has been noticed and remembered.

An important warning about appearance: The descriptive word to keep in mind is "distinctive." Gaudiness or flashiness inspires recollection, but it may be unfavorable.

Women Can Confuse Others By Changing Hair Color

Remember that woman whose name you forgot because she shifted from brunette to blonde? Or the graying lady who changed to a blue tint?

Don't confuse others and make it difficult for them to remember you by making major changes in your appearance. Find a becoming hair color and stick with it.

Remember Where You Met A Person And Remind Him Of It

In your second encounter with a person, try to remember the circumstances under which you first met him. This will be appreciated because it relieves him of struggling to remember, but it will also be a repeat stimulus-response reinforcement that will tend to anchor you in his mind.

Try to evoke images in your greeting. "Oh yes, I met you at that beautiful garden party given by the Bartons. It was last Spring and the flowers were very colorful." "We first shook hands at that conference at the Palmer House in 1970. We sat next to each other during the keynote speech."

In my personal experience, I have found that some of the skillful "successes" that were in school with me have caused me to remember them favorably because they provide me with a reminder of some school incident. Unfortunately for me, I was very active in university activities and that, coupled with an unusual name, causes them to remember me by name. But it would be impossible for me to remember all of the classmates who remember my name. If they use the technique of recalling an image or an occasion, it makes it much easier for me and, thereafter, I remember them.

It Seems To Be A Part Of Success

Almost every time that an incident arises in which people are using these techniques to assure that I remember them, I learn that they have enjoyed success in dealing with people. Most of them have risen in the business or professional world and achieved considerable success.

Make Good Use Of The "Multipliers"

In your effort to be remembered, the "multipliers" that you learned about in an earlier chapter will be very helpful. When you meet a doctor, find out about his specialty. Later in the initial meeting make some reference to it. Get the company connection of each person you meet and make some reinforcement of that to help him remember you. There are many "multipliers" that you can learn quickly and easily. At a conference or meeting, ask others for information about new acquaintances that you have made. Where is his home town? What does his company manufacture?

Feed back this information at least once before you go your separate ways and you'll find that you'll be remembered.

A Successful "Experiment" In Being Remembered

In psychology we are always thinking up little experiments that will prove an important point. In anticipation of this portion of this book, I tried this out at a resort in Hawaii. We knew none of the people at the Hana Ranch Hotel, a quiet and peaceful resort on the east coast of the Island of Maui, The guests came from all over the mainland and from all walks of life.

Our first night at Hana was a special event—a barbecue at which we all had a wonderful beef meal across the swimming pool from a small stage on which the hotel staff of native Hawaiians performed an authenic old Hawaiian musicale after dinner.

For the six couples who were nearest us, I made it a point to learn the location of their home towns. My plan was to make this a "multiplier" to see how effective this technique might be in getting others to remember me.

Since we all ate lunch and dinner together in the Hotel and it was winter on the mainland, I looked through the newspaper list of weather reports and temperatures for mainland cities until I found the temperature for each of their home towns, each day. As I saw them at lunch or dinner, I would pass each table and say: "You're sure lucky. The low was 12 degrees last night in Detroit (or Chicago, New York, Philadelphia, St. Louis, or Portland). It was 21 in Wichita."

The experiment worked: Three of these couples who saw us getting ready to leave after lunch on the following Sunday came up to us in the lobby to say, "Oh, you're leaving to go back to the cold in Wichita," or some such remark. They called us by name.

But we were even more surprised two days later at Mauna Kea Beach on the Island of Hawaii when two more of those couples went out of their way to greet us at Mauna Kea. One of them called out to me: "Hey, Barnabas, what's the temperature in Wichita today?" When I looked around it was the husband of one of those couples. He had just stopped at Mauna Kea for lunch. Another couple came up to us in the main lobby to greet us and, again, they knew our names, our home town—and made a remark about the temperature.

Very Important For Salesmen

A salesman should strive to be remembered in order to get repeat business. Also, if he is remembered in his initial contacts he will get referral sales and people will look him up when they are in a buying mood.

A schoolmate of mine is one of the most successful automobile salesmen that I know of. As a matter of fact, he is so successful that he has consistently refused management positions. He makes more money as a salesman!

Yet this man has a single phrase that never allows any of us to forget him and his occupation. Instead of saying "Good-bye" when he leaves a group or terminates a casual conversation, he always says: "Well, . .gotta go sell another Chevy!" This has some humorous advantage if he's leaving a party at midnight—but that doesn't bother him. If someone is "new" and never heard him say it before, there's another answer. If he is challenged with some statement such as: "At this hour of the night?" He replies: "Well, maybe in the morning." Or, "Sure, it's always a good time to buy a Chevy."

To Get The Most Out Of This Chapter

Follow this check list to see if you are doing the things that will make you remembered by others:

1. Do I mention my name clearly when I meet a new person?
2. Does my handshake have strength and warmth?
3. Do I use my first name? Do I have a way to keep from being called "Mister," "Mrs.," or "Miss?"
4. Is there something distinctive that I can add to my name to be sure it is remembered—spelling, history of the name, occupation, nickname?
5. Can I dream up some special words and phrases that are mine and mine alone or related to my occupation?
6. Is my dress distinctive, yet in good taste?
7. Can I add something distinctive to my handshake?

8. Do I remind people of the circumstances under which we first met?

9. Do I use "multipliers" to show that I have knowledge of a person's background?

Finally, conduct an experiment the next time you meet a group of people from different places at a conference or meeting. Make some reference to their home town. Then watch to see how they remember you, certainly and surely!

Chapter Fourteen

BE SURE THEY ARE
"READING YOU LOUD AND CLEAR"

In radio transmission the voice of the sender is frequently heard to say: "Are you reading me?" If the transmission is good, the reply comes: "Reading you loud and clear."

In this case, "loud" means adequate volume, enough that it can be heard within the limits of the volume control and above the level of any interference. "Clear" is really the important word—the transmission is understandable, not garbled or intermittent.

Make Your Transmissions "Loud and Clear"

To be sure that your work in dealing with people is effective, you need to be sure that your message comes through "loud and clear." This does not mean "loud" in the sense of raising your voice to a high volume level, but simply that it is adequate to be heard clearly within the limits of human hearing differences. "Clear" does not have the same meaning that we think of in radio transmissions, but means that what you say is understood by the person you seek to influence.

If They Don't Understand, They Can't ACT

If the people you deal with do not understand what you want them to do, they cannot act on it. Your goal is action, not aquiescence. Action can only follow from full understanding.

How To Be Sure They Hear What You Say

There are certain fundamentals about speech that derive from the study of physics. Speech starts with vibrations of the vocal chords and is "shaped" by the way in which the air passing from your lungs, past your vocal chords and through your mouth, is controlled. Your vocal chords vibrate faster when you sound a high note (such as when you say a long E—EEE), more slowly when you sound a low note (such as a long A—AY).

The "shaping" of a meaningful word takes place as the air passes through your mouth after (and while) the vocal chords vibrate. For example, look in the mirror and say "am." You have sounded a short "a" and closed your lips to terminate the sound. Now say the word "are" as you look in the mirror. You have made a similar vibration of the vocal chords, but your lips have remained open and you have raised the center of your tongue toward (but not to) the roof of your mouth. Now say the word "and." You have made the same "a" sound, but you have gradually moved your tongue to the roof of your mouth and shut off the air when you sounded the "d."

Look At People When You Talk To Them

People will understand you if you look at them as you talk. They can see the movement of your lips and even your tongue. Make sure that they don't mistake "am" for "and."

This becomes especially important with the sounds that are called "sibilants." These are the sounds like "s," "t," and "f," where the air passes rather rapidly between the tongue, teeth, and lips to make the sound. The sibilants range into the higher vibration levels (called cycles per second) and may be more difficult for persons with some hearing loss to understand. They can't misunderstand you if they see how your lips and tongue are working in relation to your teeth and the passing air.

Sound Is Directional, Too

Another reason for pointing your voice at the person you are dealing with stems from the fact that sound has some directional bearing. Your mouth points one way and the sound has more volume in the direction toward which it is pointed.

And It Holds Attention

You're more likely to "lose" a person if you turn away, not only because he may not hear you as clearly, but also because your eyes tend to hold his attention.

Get into the habit of thinking that there is a microphone between you and the other person. As with a microphone, if you turn away, you'll lose the amplification.

Enunciate Clearly

We could also sum this up by adding: Clear enunciation is important to understanding and attention. It helps your stimulus to come through "loud and clear." Get out of the habit of dropping "g's" and terminal "d's." You might be talking to a well-educated foreigner like the Frenchman who asked me: "What is the word 'dropninonous'? I can't find it in the dictionary." I said there was no such word. Then he explained that a friend of his had said he could not confer with him on Sunday because his wife's folks were 'dropninonous.' I explained that he meant they were "dropping in on us." He thought they must have had some kind of disease!

Make Your "Visual Aids" Clear

If you are coupling your word presentation with a visual stimulus, be sure it is legible. On a blackboard or chart easel, it is best not to use handwriting. Print the letters. Label the points in a diagram. Print the letters large enough to be seen at any point in the room.

If you are closer to the person addressed, as when you are working across a desk, move around to his side so that the things you print on a pad are close to him. If you are pointing to a product folder or a descriptive illustration, be sure that it is near enough to him that he can see it.

Don't Forget Gestures—But Make Them Appropriate

Gestures, whether you are making a speech or just talking to one person, are valuable. They lend some visual stimulus to what you are saying. However, it is important that they agree with the point you're trying to put across.

When you are using either D-1 or D-3 (the "delays" in Chapter Nine) to make your "bridge" before opposing an idea, you can add a gesture to emphasize that it is a matter of choice or an unimportant objection by turning your palms up and moving your hands outward. At the same time, if you are finalizing a point, you can bring your hand downward and stop it quickly to add emphasis. If you did this with D-1 or D-3 you would spoil the effect!

Avoid using clenched fists in gestures. This may develop resistance because of the association of clenched fists with bellicose attitudes.

Be Cautious About "Exhortation"

Those who have developed skill in oratory or debate tend to feel that exhortation is an added tool to change human behavior. They feel that stirring words and ringing phrases may convince where lesser words or phrases fail. We hear exhortation from the pulpit. We hear it in Congressional debate. We sometimes hear it in court rooms, although there is less of it in trials today than a decade or two in the past.

Exhortation can be highly inappropriate in face-to-face situations and small groups. It is entertaining to large groups when properly larded with humor and reason. However, in an office or living room it (a) may appear ridiculous, or (b) start an argument. In any case, one outstanding psychologist has said "Exhortation is the weakest tool to change human behavior." Certainly that would indicate that it should be used with caution.

HOW TO MAKE YOUR WORDS CONVEY MEANING

Equally important in keeping your stimulus strong is the way you put words together to make an idea clear to the person you want to change. This involves vocabulary, sentence structure, the use of illustrations and examples, and the enumeration of logical sequences in points that you make.

An Extensive Vocabulary Can Be Both Good And Bad

The more extensive your vocabulary, the more versatile you will be in understanding others. If your vocabulary is limited you may not get the full meaning of something said by another person. That's the good side of having a wide vocabulary.

On the other hand, the better your vocabulary, the more tempted you are to use it. This may cause someone to miss your meaning if he does not have as good a vocabulary as you.

Research shows that there is a marked relationship between vocabulary and the amount of education the person has. The high school graduate has a larger vocabulary than the average person. Keep in mind that in our country the average education is still only 10 school grades. The average college graduate has a much larger fund of words than the average high school graduate and the average executive is above the average college graduate in vocabulary.

Develop a good vocabulary in order to be sure you understand others with good vocabularies. Then use it sparingly, especially when you don't know how much education the other person has.

"Big" Words May Confuse

A salesman said, "This shipment ran into the same exigencies as your penultimate shipment."

The purchasing agent said, "Hell, we never ordered any penultimates!"

Why say "terminal objective" when "end result" is clear to everyone? Usually the word "increase" or "addition to" will do as well as "increment." Your goal is to convince, not confuse.

Get To The Point

After you have smoothed the path for your stimulus by using the techniques in Chapters Four, Five & Six, be sure that your next sentence gets right to the point. If you start with several qualifying clauses, you may "lose" your listener. He may start to think about something else. He may try to anticipate what you're going to try to get him to do. In either case, you're weakening your power.

Let's take two ways of expressing an idea: You want to emphasize that the important thing is "cost." We'll show a good and a bad way to do it.

Bad: "While there are other factors, some of them big and some comparatively insignificant—with varying aspects and phases—let me point out that the main and basic element is cost." Why is this bad? There are three clauses that precede the main idea. Even the technique of seeming to ask permission "let me point out" has lost it's value because it is preceded by the qualifying clauses. Coming late, it may not be noticed.

Good: "As you have indicated earlier, the main factor is cost. While there are other factors. . ." In this example, the technique (relating the idea to his previous position) is immediately followed by the point you want to make—cost. If it is really necessary to introduce the qualifying phrases and alternatives, let them come after the main idea, not before.

Use The Right Type Of Sentence

Those who have studied the fundamentals of good writing recognize that there are three types of sentences, each with its own special purpose. While this book is not designed to teach expertness in writing, there are reference books which will let you dig more deeply into the types of sentences and their uses. We will summarize here.

The *periodic* sentence is one in which the meaning is not complete until the end of the sentence—the "period." It is usually short: "In its class, our car is the lowest-priced." Another: "The thing we are most concerned with is cost." The periodic sentence is best used for emphasis. It should either precede what you have to say or act as a summary at the end. It is usually simple and to-the-point.

The *loose* sentence is somewhat nondescript. It is described as a sentence in which a period could be inserted before the end without making it incomplete as a sentence. Example: "The things which determine cost are not found just in accounting books, in the analyses made by engineers, in pricing formulas, or in textbooks on methods." The loose sentence is most useful for presenting a sequence or a series.

The *balanced* sentence may also be a loose sentence. The term "balanced" derives from its value in submitting clauses of equal value or alternatives. It is especially useful to place two ideas in juxtaposition or to offer sharpness of contrast.

An example of a good use of the balanced sentence might come from our concepts of "cost." "The cost of a process or product may be calculated from actual research or it may come from a disciplined estimate made by someone with actual experience."

Use All Three Types Of Sentences

The over-use of periodic sentences may make your conversation sound dull and monotonous. Too many loose sentences have a confusing effect—the added clauses may confuse. We will not normally find frequent uses for the balanced sentence because of its special nature.

Use the periodic sentence to open or close, to announce or summarize your idea.

Use the loose sentence where you have a sequence of ideas.

Use the balanced sentence for contrasting thoughts or for alternatives.

For holding interest, use all three in appropriate ways.

When You Use Sequences, Try To Number Them

If your idea involves a sequence of ideas or a series of alternatives, try to assign numbers or letters to them. "We've got three ways to go. Number 1—We can send Charlie to see this customer. Number 2—I can write him a nice letter. Number 3—We might just drop the matter entirely."

There are a lot of ways of enumerating. You can say "a," "b," or "c," "in the first place, in the second place," etc., or even "x," "y," and "z."

Use Colorful Words, Not Drab Words

As a part of your power, learn to express your ideas with bright, colorful words rather than drab and dull words. If you say, "I'm glad you like it," your words are not nearly as interesting as if you say, "I'm not only grateful, but complimented that you like it." Learn to use words such as "fired up," or "challenged" instead of just "pleased" or "motivated."

Try To Avoid Clichés And Trite Phrases

Part of the "spark" that produces power in dealing with people is re-phrasing old adages or "saws" into fresh phrases. "Practice makes perfect" can be made "The more you do it the better you do it." Instead of saying: "Please repeat that, I didn't get it," a friend of mine says: "Pitch that one closer to the plate and I'll swing at it." "Penny wise and pound foolish" can become "You might save a nickel and lose a dollar."

Use Illustrations And Examples

One of the best ways to be sure that your words convey meaning is the use of illustrations and examples. The techniques of presenting ideas and opposing ideas included some mention of this. We showed in one of the techniques of presenting an idea or attitude "the consequences of failure" to accept it. The use of examples and "for instances" goes beyond that.

Make it a rule: Whenever you can cite an example of the idea you want to put over, you will make it clearer. Concentrate on thinking of appropriate illustrations and examples.

Bring Your Illustrations Close To The Other Person

Your examples and illustrations will be still more powerful if they fit the background of experience—the conditioning—of the other person. Occasionally this may produce a "magic" multiplier, as in Chapter Three. If you know you have a football fan and you want to express futility, you can use a current league-leader and say: "That's like trying to beat the (undefeated team). It doesn't happen very often." Or if you're trying to overcome skepticism, you might say: "Nobody thought the (name of Cinderella team) could win it all."

Use "Figures Of Speech"

Illustrations and examples can be quite lengthy and drawn from parallel circumstances or they can be "figures of speech.' Figures of speech are ways to express an idea without actually expressing it overtly. The two you need to use in developing power to deal with people are the *simile* and the *metaphor.*

The metaphor expresses something as *like* something else. "It's like 1929"; "He drinks like W. C. Fields"; "She's as pretty as Raquel Welch." The metaphor simply states the similarity without the word such as "like" or "as." "In terms of inflation, it's 1929"; "He's W. C. Fields when it comes to drinking"; "She's Raquel Welch when it comes to looks."

Figures of speech can cushion your objections, too. If you want to indicate skepticism, you can say: "I'm a doubting Thomas." Or you could say: "That's like trying to collect an account from a bankrupt," or "It's as tough as getting an audience with the President."

To Get The Most Out Of This Chapter

Remember: to get action in dealing with people, your Stimulus must come through "loud and clear." Good enunciation, looking directly at another person, and using appropriate visual aids are all helpful.

After you have used your introductory technique (as learned from earlier chapters), get right to the point. Don't put a "fog" of clauses ahead of your idea. It may cause you to "lose" the other person.

Stand in front of a mirror and repeat the alphabet. Note how the position of your tongue, lips and teeth changes with the sounding of each letter. Read a familiar passage such as Lincoln's Gettysburg Address, enunciating each word clearly as you look in the mirror.

Select a series of words with final "g's"—"going," "hearing," "driving," etc. Sound the final "g" clearly.

If you have a tape recorder, read or recite a familiar passage as rapidly as you can. Then listen to see how many syllables you have dropped or elided, how many final sounds you have omitted.

Write three examples of each of the three types of sentences.

Make a list of ten people that you know. Then think of an illustration or example that will be especially clear to each person because of something you know about him that is different.

Make a list of ten common adages or "saws." Rephrase them in different, modern language. Start with "He who hesitates is lost" and "Haste makes waste."

Write ten similes ("It's like...") and change each to a metaphor.

Ask a close friend, your wife, husband, etc. if you have any bad habits that tend to make your expressions of ideas less clear than they should be. Also find out if you have any "pet" words that are not understandable to some of your friends.

Chapter Fifteen

ATTITUDES THAT BUILD
YOUR POWER

It has been my good fortune to work closely with many individuals who have developed Power in dealing with people. Many of them are chief executives who built great businesses because of their skill in motivating others. In addition, there are civic and community leaders and men and women at the intermediate levels of management.

Are there differences in their attitudes which gave them more Power? Do those without such attitudes show weaknesses in dealing with people?

The answer to both questions is "Yes." In this chapter we will describe some of those differences in attitudes because it will help to condition you toward the strength they possessed.

They Have An "Accelerator" And A "Brake"

In one of the first research studies which I made of successful executives and leaders, I discovered an unusual combination of

two personality traits. I discussed the findings with a psychologist who was particularly skilled in the interpretation of such
traits. "Why do these successful men show restlessness and
impatience, yet at the same time manifest a tendency to be
tense and anxious in face-to-face situations?"

The answer was brief and to the point: "They have an
'accelerator' to keep them driving forward, and a 'brake' to
keep them under control."

Their eagerness to "get the job done" was expressed on the
test as "manic" tendency—the desire to want to get things done
(yesterday?).

This was the "accelerator."

Their caution and restraint—their "brake"—was reflected on
the test by the "bottling up" of their energy in order to
maintain control in face-to-face situations.

Failures: An "Accelerator" Without A "Brake"

Later, when I was able to get a research group of greater
numbers, the successful group still showed the "accelerator"
and the "brake." I made a contrasting study of a sizeable group
of men who had failed to develop Power to deal with people.

The difference was quite clear. The failures had the accelerator, to be sure. But instead of a "brake" they had a "free-
wheeling" tendency. Their responses to the test indicated a
resistance to discipline, an inner revolt against the rules and
codes required of social living.

How This Relates To Power To Deal With People

The successful personalities had *control* of their inner horsepower. Despite their inner drive to "get things done," they were
able to avoid irritating others, to prevent others from turning
against them. They approached face-to-face situations with
caution, even though they learned (see below) not to put them
off, not to procrastinate.

"Control" Is The Key Word

When angered, the successes did not show it (or made
apologies for it if they did). They were willing to go to the

trouble to use techniques such as you have learned. If they were impatient, they did not communicate it to others.

Like a powerful automobile, they had the motivation to move forward rapidly. But along with it they had good steering and power brakes!

"Control" But Not "Delay"

For them "control" did not mean "delay," however. In talking with over 200 such successful people I found that a great majority had developed the habit of dealing with the "people" situations first. "If you put off the problems with people, they get bigger. It is the people problems which I put at the top of my list." Another said: "People problems get bigger if you let them go longer. I sleep better if I've taken care of them." Still another said: "When I've got a problem with a person who's some distance away, I pick up the telephone and call him. It's expensive—but it doesn't cost as much as a festering misunderstanding. And it's cheaper than psychiatry."

Maturity In Facing The Unexpected

Those who develop Power to deal with people have a maturity that causes them to feel a sense of readiness for the unusual, the unexpected.

Sometimes we must expect an objection to an idea we are attempting to put across. We often know, from knowing a person, whether he tends to react that way. More often, however, the objection or the wrong attitude is not predictable. We do not have access to sufficient knowledge about the other person or have not known him long enough to make him predictable. The negative attitude, the objection, or resistance comes as a surprise.

Those who have Power in dealing with people don't let such unexpected obstacles to their stimulus create panic over-concern. They have a maturity that has taught them to expect the unexpected, to be ready for it.

Yet this sense of "readiness" is not a gesture of futility. It is

not accompanied by any self-sympathy. People who are successful in dealing with people do not feel a sense of resignation
when faced with the unexpected. They have a sense of readiness
without any feeling of being resigned to their "fate."

This is the maturity needed to succeed in dealing with
people.

How The Techniques Help

In my work with younger men in supervision and management, I have found that careful study and practice of the
techniques of opposing negative attitudes or objections helps to
develop this sense of readiness. You studied these in Chapters
Seven, Eight, Nine, and Ten. Once a person has learned how to
remove the other person's feeling of blame for his opposing idea
or attitude, once he has learned how to make the "bridge" to
overcome such opposition, he feels more comfortable, more
"ready." One young supervisor said: "You know, since I
learned those techniques I don't let these guys in my department throw me for a loss. I don't get impatient or upset
anymore. The minute something comes up I start thinking
'which technique will be best?' and I think about how many of
them I can use. It 'cools me off' and lets me respond more
effectively."

Perseverance In Dealing With People

For years psychologists have studied a trait which the first
researchers called "Ascendancy-Submission." They described
the person who had this trait as "ascendant."

Later another group referred to the same trait as "Dominance" and developed tests which would measure it. The person
who scores above average on this trait is called "Dominant"; the
person who is below average is "Submissive."

Dominance may be a misleading word because it sounds a
great deal like "domineering." People who are most successful
in dealing with others seldom seem to "domineer" over others.
They do not employ autocratic methods. They do not use
"either/or else" tactics.

The best description of this trait is "Perseverance in Dealing With People." It can be developed with determination and effort.

Let's Go Back To Stimulus-Response

While a strong stimulus—YOU—may get a favorable response immediately, we know that you may sometimes meet with resistance. No matter how skillfully we present an idea, there is a good chance that it will meet with objection at first. When this happens, we use our "bridging" techniques to oppose objections and go right ahead with the strong stimulus.

The dominant person is the one who has more perseverance in meeting and overcoming objections skillfully. He "stays with 'em" longer.

This is what makes a great "closer" in selling. He knows (or feels) that each objection he overcomes may be the last one. It may be the "real" one that has been concealed up to now. If he stops his Power, his stimulus, his work to that point may be for nothing. If he perseveres, he will eventually close the sale.

If The Salesman Quits, His Work Helps A Competitor

A great "closer" seldom gives up or gives in. He realizes that what he has done to stimulate a buying motive will not help him get the sale if he quits half way to his goal. The prospect has been *conditioned* to a certain point. He will probably buy from a competitor if the salesman "gives up" on an objection or fails to overcome it.

If the salesman gives up, all of his work to try to get a "close" will have helped a competitor. Another salesman who has more of this trait—more "Perseverance In Dealing With People"—will close the sale.

Remember "The Case Of The Stingy Giver"

When Bill Jones interviewed Charlie Roe about his United Fund pledge (Chapter Two), he ran into a series of objections. His first obstacle was the receptionist. Then Roe tried to get rid of him. He said he would fill out the pledge card and mail it in. Then Roe objected to the large amount. Next he found fault with one of the UF agencies, and so on. But Bill Jones, a successful salesman and sales manager, skillfully disposed of the objections until he got the pledge. Unlike the earlier United Fund solicitors, he would not give up.

Bill Jones had "it"—perseverance in dealing with people. It's a desirable trait to develop. It's a part of your Power to deal with people.

Perseverance Is Not The Same As Obstinacy

The salesman must persevere. If the prospect gets away, he may buy from a competitor.

The supervisor and the person who is striving to develop Power in family or social situations is not under such a severe threat. The difficult or "problem" employee may become convinced tomorrow after thinking it over. Also, there are supervisory or social situations in which we actually are convinced that the other person has a point in his favor.

Refusal to give in when the evidence is against us is obstinacy, not perseverance.

Supervisors sometimes get good ideas toward improving departmental efficiency from the objections raised by employees who seem to be "wrong" at first.

Successful People Seek Consensus

It is characteristic of those who are successful in dealing with others that they are able to bring about group agreement—a consensus. One of the most successful production superintendents I know demonstrated this before a group of younger men in a training session.

I asked him, "Carl, if the Vice President in charge of Manufacturing called you and said they were going to have to change the production lines in your department and wanted it done by tomorrow morning, what would you do?"

He replied: "I'd get the boys together and explain th

problem. I'd ask them how we could do it. They would come up with a lot of ideas, some good and some bad. When one of them hit on the right way—or close to it—I'd agree with him. Then he and all the others would break their necks to get it done."

One of the younger men in the training group said: "But suppose nobody came up with the right idea or anything even close to it?"

Carl replied: "That's never happened in twenty-five years."

Carl was using one of the best techniques set out in Chapter Four. He was getting the other person to Express the idea so that it became his own idea, not Carl's.

Study Your Successes, Not Your Failures

Another characteristic of those who develop Power in dealing with people is their refusal to undermine their own self-confidence by brooding over their failures.

Except in the case of an obvious mistake, the salesman, the supervisor or the person in a family or social situation can never be sure as to the reason he failed to change the other person. The obvious mistakes are easy to see. If we made the mistake of starting an argument and could not stop it, we usually know it. If, for lack of information or improper use of techniques, we failed to overcome the objection or negative attitude, we usually realize it—sooner or later.

You'll Profit From Studying Your Successes

Your successes are maps which charted your path to a favorable response. As you study this book and begin to improve your Power to deal with people, you will find it helpful to study the cases in which you succeeded. If you start to brood, if you try to figure out how "that one got away," immediately change your thoughts, substitute a review of a success. Think of how this technique worked or that "multiplier" added to the strength of your stimulus.

You'll be achieving some self-conditioning, developing habits which will strengthen your Power.

To Get The Most Out Of This Chapter

Your development of Power to deal with people will be speeded by developing attitudes similar to the attitudes of successful people.

Develop control in face-to-face situations. Do not let your impatience show. However, this control does not mean delay—take care of the "people" problems promptly.

Don't let opposition "throw you into a tail spin." Be ready for the unexpected, but don't let your readiness become weakened by feelings of "giving up."

The person who has Power in dealing with people is willing to persevere, overcoming each obstacle or objection until the desired response is achieved in the form of action.

Study your successes and not your failures. In dealing with people you learn more from successes than from failures.

Think of a major purchase that you have made in recent months. Write down the objections you made before the salesman finally "closed" the sale.

Write down the names of the three persons you know who are most successful in dealing with people. Then see how many of the attitudes mentioned in this chapter seem to be possessed by them.

Answer these questions—"Yes" or "No."

1. Do I have control, caution, in face-to-face situations?
2. Does my control slow down or limit my Power to deal with people?
3. Can I meet several objections without giving up or giving in?
4. Do I think more about my successes than about my failures?

Chapter Sixteen

YOUR "PROGRAM"
TO DEVELOP POWER TO
DEAL WITH PEOPLE

Through this book you have learned how modern scientific knowledge can help you develop power to deal with people.

You have studied some of the fundamentals of behavior and how to change it. You have studied how to strengthen your stimulus in five different ways, including how to multiply the power of your stimulus. You have learned techniques that will smooth the pathway for your ideas and techniques to bridge to your opposition of negative ideas. You have learned how to make your stimulus "loud and clear," and have seen the attitudes that characterize those who succeed.

Your Final Need: A "Program" For You

Modern science has established that the human brain and central nervous system is actually a grand computer that dwarfs in size and capability any computer ever created by man. With its ten billion relays and thousands of connections, it has tremendous capability. Size (in terms of relay numbers) is not the only difference between the capability of the human mind and that of a wire-and-transistor computer. The mechanical computer must be "programmed" by a human being. Without such a program, it is useless. But the human brain and central nervous system has its own "programmer." The frontal lobe of the brain can "program" the other portions of the brain and nervous system.

Your final step in developing power to deal with people is to create your "program."

"It's Not A Part-Time Job"

The statement: "It's not a part-time job" is the first instruction to feed into your own "computer." You must learn to use your Power in all situations involving people.

Don't let yourself think of power to deal with people as something that you can "turn on and turn off." This does not mean that you will always get others to do what you want them to do. Don't expect perfection. But even when you are "outvoted" or are unable to change someone, don't be a Mr. Milquetoast. Let's look at an example.

Be Gracious, But Not Submissive

Suppose your social "crowd" is trying to decide what to do on a certain Saturday night. You would rather stay home to watch a favorite television movie, but the crowd wants to go to hear a visiting "name" band. Eventually, you realize that more of them want to go to the dance. You do not want to be stubborn or obstinate. Do you remain silent?

No. You do not simply "give in."

Do you try to change them? Not unless it is very important to you.

To keep yourself properly "programmed," you say something like this: "Well, I'd rather stay home and watch television, but I'll go along with the gang."

This one remark, in good tact and friendliness, keeps your "program" intact. It does not erode your personal Power.

Express Your Opposition, Then Cooperate

Whether it involves a committee, a team, or a decision at your work, make it clear that just because you don't agree with the decision does not mean that you won't work hard for the majority decision.

Keep your own integrity intact by stating your "minority" opinion, then work hard for the project the majority has adopted. The main thing is that you have kept your own inner "program" satisfied by expressing your individuality.

Build An "Image" In Your Mind—Then Live It!

Another part of your personal "program" is erecting the image in your mind of a person who is successful in dealing with people. This need not be a single individual whom you happen to know or admire, it may be a composite. You should be able to "see" this person in your mind. This person does the things that we have talked about in this book. Of course, if you are a short person, your "image" cannot be tall. This person must be YOU in terms of physical attributes. But within the physical limits this image is a person who is a powerful YOU.

As You Build Your "Image" Study People Who Have Power

Look around you. Who do you know who has developed power to deal with people? What can you do that he does?

Watch the people who show skill in selling you something you did not ask for. Study the people who are able to rally a committee behind them. Observe how the top people in your business or occupation use their skills to get people to do what they want them to do.

Watch For "Low Pressure" Skills

Don't be misled into thinking that the only persons whose manners and methods are worth adopting are those who are overpowering—"high pressure." Often you will see that people develop power with "low pressure" methods—a soft voice, a gentle manner, a seeming shyness. This is coupled with good technique and careful study of those they seek to influence.

A Negro clerk at Sears, using a very soft voice and a very self-effacing approach, succeeded in selling me a radial-arm saw that I had no intention of buying when I went in to buy some cadmium-plated bolts. His questioning was skillful and he was alert to everything I said. Soon he found a "multiplier" and that was all he needed.

One of the best insurance counselors that I know is very mild-mannered. One of the most influential lobbyists I ever met was a very quiet person, seemingly non-gregarious.

Don't Be A "Door-Mat"

Some books and some writers concentrate so heavily on the ways to keep people from disliking you that they seem to want you to become a "door-mat" and let people walk over you. This is not good for you. We mentioned the case of the young supervisor who had been led into this error in a college course called "Human Relations."

Your "program" demands that you develop individuality as an integral part of developing power to deal with people.

Build An Image That Fits YOU

Your "program" does not involve the building of an image that runs counter to your nature. You must be yourself. The "program" is designed to make you your *best* YOU when it comes to dealing with people.

If you are naturally an unsociable, non-gregarious person, don't make the mistake of trying to appear to be the "life of the party." This will show through. It will appear artificial. On the other hand, if you are unsociable, you want to make a special effort to study people very carefully. If you learn a lot about them, they will think you are friendly whether you are or not! Your knowledge of them will come through "loud and clear" as you work to get them to do things.

On the other hand, if you are a sociable, gregarious person, remember that this can interfere with your effectiveness. You can become so absorbed with liking people that you lose sight of your goal—which is to change them toward your aims, your goals. You must remember especially the need for perseverance in dealing with people. Equally important, you must remember what we said in Chapter Fourteen about getting to the point quickly, avoiding qualifying clauses and wasting time with "small talk."

"Get Involved"

An important aspect of your "program" is getting yourself into situations which give you a chance to practice the things you're learning in this book. The best phrase to describe this is: "Get Involved!"

Just as people are conditioned by the actions they take to satisfy a need, so you need to accomplish some "self-conditioning." In addition to your study of this book, it will take some practice on your part to get the "program" set in your mind.

This may create a problem for you if you are not already a salesman, supervisor, or community leader. You will need to find situations in which you must put across your ideas and be ready to overcome opposition to them.

To help you remember this:

One problem is solved
If you "get involved."

It's Easy To "Get Involved"

Your community, your company, your church, your lodge, your union, your health-and-welfare organizations, your Chamber of Commerce—all of these groups are eagerly looking for leaders.

To be sure, you won't become President of an organization or Chairman of a Board of Directors at the start. You have to "work your way up."

You Can Start With Committee Assignments

The various committees of your Chamber of Commerce, your

church, and your lodge are crying for leadership. If you expose yourself to service, you'll soon be asked to assume some leadership. Even as a committee member you have an opportunity to influence the rest of the committee to your way of thinking, using the tools you have learned in this book.

In communities where there is a United Fund or other organization devoted to united giving, the organizations that are beneficiaries tend to lose leadership because they are not required to raise money annually. An organization such as a Red Cross Chapter or a Mental Health Association gets a "shot in the arm" each year when they campaign for funds. If this is not needed, there is a tendency for the leadership to deteriorate. Executive Directors of such organizations recognize this. If you approach one of them about serving on a committee, he'll welcome you with open arms. You'll get a chance to get involved—and quickly!

Get Involved With Fund Raising

Most people dislike asking people for money, yet this is one of the surest ways to get some practice in dealing with people. Your United Fund is looking for volunteers every year as the time for the campaign comes around.

Unless you already have some practice, start easy. Work on smaller assignments—employee groups and small givers—before you tackle the big gifts section.

Volunteer to work with your church in its member canvass to raise its budget. Set a goal for yourself—to get a certain percentage of increase from the cards that you handle.

Join Up!

One way to get involved is to join some group that has something about it that excites you. Perhaps it's a camera club or even an investment club. Lodges are looking for leaders. Find something that you think you enjoy and "join up."

Your Growth Will Be Gradual

Don't expect to develop your full Power in a few days. As

you try the techniques and methods explained here you will see how well they work. This will give you some real satisfaction, increase your feeling of personal worth. Then, as you tackle problems that are a little bigger—as you become the chairman of a committee, the head of a United Fund campaign section, are elected to the Board of Directors of an organization—you'll be able to see how your own growth has resulted from practice.

Continue "Conditioning" Yourself

Psychologists say that each time we repeat a stimulus-response activity in satisfaction of a need, we are making a "reinforcement." This is "conditioning" as mentioned in Chapter Two. It is what makes habit. In this case it is what makes Power to deal with people. It sets your "program" in your mind.

Reinforcing Is Easy

You will get reinforcement of your Power each time you work with another person or group and find that your efforts accomplished something.

However, you can also add reinforcement to your development if you review this book regularly. One way to do this is to have a copy of the book on your bedside table or by your easy chair. Review parts of it every two or three days. Glance through the exercises at the end of each chapter. Repeat some of them.

Review The Techniques—Check Them Off

At the end of Chapters Four through Six are technique check lists for presenting ideas. As you review each of those chapters, make a check mark in front of a technique that you have used successfully.

Do this with the techniques described in Chapters Seven through Ten—the techniques of "bridging" between the expression of a wrong idea and your opposition to it, the techniques you need to overcome opposition to your ideas. Check them off as you use them.

When you have done this for a few weeks, go back through these chapters looking for techniques that you have *not* used, the ones that you have not checked. Make a special effort to find situations in which you can try them out.

"Bedside" Reinforcements

Sometimes you'll find it hard to get to sleep. Other times you may wake up at night. If you have a pad and a pencil at your bedside you can get additional reinforcement by jotting down ideas about people you have worked with recently. And you can plan your program for people that you're going to work with soon.

Make Your "Program" A "Way Of Life"

Perhaps you will be able to remember your need for a continuing "program" if we give you a few lines of rhyme to help you remember, to remind you of the need to make continuous reinforcements and help you to make your Power to deal with people a part of your life. It will actually become a "Way of Life" for you.

> *"Program" yourself to use your Power*
> *Every week, every day, every waking hour;*
> *"Program" yourself—everything that you do*
> *Should match the image of a powerful "YOU."*

To Get The Most Out Of This Chapter

Remember: Just as people are "conditioned" by what has happened to them, so you can "condition" yourself. Conscious effort in the form of a "Program" will be the final phase of developing your Power to deal with people.

Developing your Power to deal with people is not a "part-time" job. It involves continuous alertness. It requires the exploitation of each opportunity to lead, to influence others. Even when you "go along" with the "crowd" you should tactfully express your opposition.

You will build an "image" of the person you want to be and then live that image. The "image" should fit you, not run counter to your physical attributes or your personality.

You need opportunities to get "practice" in dealing with people. The answer to this is to "get involved." Serve on committees, join organizations.

Continuously reinforce your "Program." Review this book, repeat the exercises, check off the techniques, make notes about people.

Make a list of fraternal, civic, educational or "hobby" groups that you might join. Study them over and decide which one or ones will give you the best chance to practice your techniques for developing power to deal with people.

Get a list of the United Fund agencies or non-United Fund agencies in your community. Study over them and decide which ones might give you opportunity to serve and exercise leadership.

Memorize the four-line verse in the last paragraph of this chapter.

MORE POWER TO YOU!

INDEX

233